PENCERRIG

Statue of Thomas Jones, Temple Gardens, Llandrindod Wells

PENCERRIG
and its past families

by
Penelope Bourdillon

Illustrations by
Marcia Gibson-Watt

By the same Authors

The Four Graces

A.C.T.S. 1

Hope in the Valley
(A Companion in Times of Bereavement)

Also by Penelope Bourdillon

How God can Peel an Onion

A bun dance

Rhymes without Reason

Published by Greyhound Self-Publishing 2023
Malvern, Worcestershire, United Kingdom.

Printed and bound by Aspect Design
89 Newtown Road, Malvern, Worcs. WR14 1PD
United Kingdom
Tel: 01684 561567
E-mail: allan@aspect-design.net
Website: www.aspect-design.net

A copy of this book has been deposited with the British Library Board.

Cover photo by Deb Carrel ©

ISBN: 978-1-915803-03-0

I dedicate this book to
Marcia Gibson-Watt, Sarah Herbert-Jones and Angela Yardley,
the originators of the Thomas Jones Pencerrig Trust, CIC.,
who are working tirelessly for this important house to be restored
to its former glory and to be saved for the nation of Wales.

Contents

PART TWO

LIST OF ILLUSTRATIONS

ACKNOWLEDGEMENTS

We would like to express our thanks to all those who have kindly provided information to research the Pencerrig story. These are too numerous to name individually, but my gratitude cannot be expressed enough to Tanya Jenkins whose knowledge of local history and of Nonconformism and Dissent has been invaluable, and for all her help; and to Robin Gibson-Watt who has been patient and supportive throughout. Also my son Patrick who knows a great deal more about his ancestors than I do, and for allowing us to reproduce pictures and portraits from his collection, and my heartfelt thanks go to Rob Loveridge for his expertise, patience and encouragement.

We would also like to thank the National Museum of Wales for their permission to reproduce Francesco Renaldi's Conversation Piece, and the National Gallery in London who have given permission to use 'The Wall in Naples' by Thomas Jones, also The National Library of Wales for permission to use some of the pictures from his Sketch Books.

I want to make it quite clear that this in no way set out to be an academic work, but simply a personal view of what I have heard, read and gleaned over the years about the remarkable Clara Thomas, sometimes called the Lady of Llwyn Madoc. I have tried to give, as far as I am able, a personal viewpoint, because I had the pleasure and privilege of talking to people who had met or remembered her, when I first came to Llwyn Madoc over sixty years ago.

I have worked from various different sources, mostly family, and some may be not entirely accurate: for this reason there are no references or footnotes, and I apologise profusely for any mistakes. It is not intended in any way to be a reference book, and I hope it will be enjoyed more as a lightweight account rather than a definitive history of the great lady; her family; Pencerrig; and some of the events that happened there and at Llwyn Madoc.

However if you want to learn a great deal more about Miss Thomas I would like to suggest that you get a copy of a newly published book: *Clara Thomas (1841-1914 Boneddige Haelionus / Philanthropist* by *Huw Thomas Davies*. It became apparent to him that this remarkable lady was worthy of further research which would illuminate how she came to be recognised and described as a 'Local Benefactress', 'Philanthropist', and a 'Great Lady Lost to Breconshire'. Much of the material found needed to be reinvestigated, brought together into one account of a remarkable individual, and sources clearly identified. I commend this book to you for further reading.

PART ONE

Chapter 1

INTRODUCTION TO MISS CLARA THOMAS (1841-1914) and THE LINK BETWEEN PENCERRIG and LLWYN MADOC

To understand about Pencerrig it is important to know about a very remarkable lady called Clara Thomas. She is of particular

Miss Clara Thomas as a young woman

interest because she not only inherited the Pencerrig estate from her mother's side of the family, but also the Llwyn Madoc estate where I lived for over forty years. I very soon learned about this close link between the two houses, which I feel is not only pertinent but essential to the history of Pencerrig.

I hope this will become clear as the story unfolds. You will also find many links to several other local houses which I hope will also be of interest.

In 1961 I married one of the descendants of Miss Thomas' family, Mervyn Bourdillon, and we had the pleasure and privilege of living at Llwyn Madoc. What a wonderful place it was to bring up a family. My mother-in-law (born Cara Phyllis Evan-Thomas) always referred to Clara Thomas as Granny, which may seem odd as she (Clara) was unmarried and had no direct descendants. Miss Thomas, as I shall call her, because that is how

I have always heard spoken of her, had brought up Lilian, one of her Lee cousins from Ireland. This girl subsequently married another cousin, Algernon Thomas and they were my mother-in-law (Cara Phyllis)'s parents, so you can see why she considered Miss Thomas her grandmother. [Algernon, incidentally, was the first Chairman of Breconshire County Council.]

I hope you will agree that this, below, is a delightful introduction to Miss Thomas, taken from the book 'Squires of South Wales' by Herbert M Vaughan. There is a chapter entitled **The Lady of Llwyn Madoc** and here is an excerpt from it:

'Kindness and sympathy beamed from her face; she had, I think, the sweetest smile I have ever seen on a human countenance. She was as humble as she was holy, but nevertheless she owned a strong will of her own'.

'A lively and very beautiful lady, she spent an exceptionally full public life of works and hospitality, culture and virtue. However, in spite of her prodigious wealth her daily life was plain and wholesome.'

There is so much more, as you will discover later, but let us have a quick look at the significance of a little trolley, which was found in the outbuildings at Llwyn Madoc by Mr. Geoffrey Bright of Russell, Baldwin and Bright, now known as Brightwells. He used to come to stay at Llwyn Madoc with my husband's uncle; he loved all the local happenings and wrote many short stories about them, which I and many of our visitors over the years have always enjoyed reading. He wrote this:

THE LITTLE TROLLEY

'I never travel along the twelve miles of road from Builth Wells to Beulah and Llanwrtyd Wells without thinking of how it has improved since I first knew it. It is now a wide tarmacadamed thoroughfare with lay-bys equipped with litter bins, corners with wide grass verges, and bridges and culverts over fast flowing streams, reconstructed and widened to give ample visibility ahead.

'The second reason is that I am always reminded about a quaint little four-wheeled trolley that I discovered years ago in the outbuildings of a large country house near Beulah. I was staying in this house, Llwyn Madoc, with Commander and Mrs. Charles Evan-Thomas in the 1950s, and that odd little vehicle had me guessing. 'My host supplied the answer…

'The trolley had belonged to his aunt, from whom he had inherited Llwyn Madoc, and his aunt was none other than the well beloved Victorian Squireen of North Breconshire, whose generosity and good works still linger in the memory of the older folk and that delectable part of Wales.

'Miss Clara Thomas is now almost a legend. She owned two large estates, Llwyn Madoc near Beulah, and Pencerrig near Builth. She was very rich, a model landlord, and a fairy 'godmother' to all in need in that remote district, which in her day was almost feudal. Her daily life was conducted on old fashioned Christian principles.

'She spent half the year at Llwyn Madoc, that lovely rambling old house near Beulah, snuggling against a rounded hill, and still lovingly cared for I'm glad to say; and the rest of the year at Pencerrig, just two miles beyond Builth on the Llandrindod road, a smart stone built Victorian mansion. Pencerrig was only about five miles from the then fashionable resort of Llandrindod, where in her heyday the 'haute monde' repaired to for their holidays; this enabled her to entertain her friends and take part in the assemblies and other 'goings on' in Llandrindod.

'Now we come to this odd little vehicle. Every year, in early summer, a cavalcade wound its way from Pencerrig to Llwyn Madoc; at the head of the column was the landau conveying Miss Clara and her life-long friend Miss Gertrude Lewis Lloyd.

'Next came a four-wheeled brake, filled to capacity by the household staff. Behind this was a two-wheeled heavy spring cart with the hand luggage (the heavy luggage had gone on before) – then **the little trolley loaded with the grand pianoforte**, and the rear of the column was brought up by the house cows in charge of the cowman and his young assistant.

'The little procession traversed that twelve miles at a walking pace. No doubt travellers in traps or on horseback gave it right of way, and I would think that the police in Builth, who most certainly had been warned, would see that it had a clear passage through the narrow streets of the old market town.

'Only fifty years ago! Within the memory of many of us. What a shock those large lorries would get today if they saw 'that lot' suddenly converging on them round one of these recently widened corners, especially the grand piano mounted on the low trolley.'

When I first lived at Llwyn Madoc I loved talking to a dear lady, Mrs. Powell, who lived at Maendu which is on the main road just as you come into Beulah; she would tell me how excited all the children were when Miss Thomas and her entourage returned to Llwyn Madoc each spring. They were given the day off school, and the people in the village used to line the route, AND the girls were allowed to wear their best dresses on this auspicious day. She could remember it vividly all those years later, and as she recounted it to me I felt that she almost relived the excitement she had as a small child.

Next is a thumbnail sketch of Miss Thomas which sets the scene into which she suddenly found herself at the age of twenty two because she had also inherited the Llanbradach estate from her father. It was taken from an article in a South Wales newspaper written by a Mr Dennis Sellwood many years ago:

'More than a hundred years ago, coal was discovered deep under Tynygraig Farm, two miles to the north of Caerphilly. The land belonged to Miss Clara Thomas, a wealthy heiress. Her ancestors

A very early picture with Llwyn Madoc in the distance
by Thomas Jones

Pencerrig and the Stable Block 1760

had farmed this part of the Rhymney Valley for several centuries. As the coalmining village of Llanbradach came into being, Miss Clara Thomas took a keen interest in all aspects of its development: the National School, housing and the layout of streets, the provision of a public hall and a park; also, being a devout Anglican, early on she reserved a plot of land for the church. At her own expense, a handsome building soon sprang up and was dedicated as All Saints on 2nd June 1897, but it was not fully completed until 1909.

'Miss Thomas, whose cousin Ellen lived with her husband Colonel Morgan Lindsay in Ystrad Fawr House, Ystrad Mynach, regularly visited the district until her death in June 1914. A party of miners attended the burial in the little churchyard near Llwyn Madoc, her Brecon home; and a Memorial service was held at All Saints, Llanbradach a few days later.

'Even though Miss Thomas divided her time between two large country houses, Llwyn Madoc and Pencerrig, both in north Breconshire, she was also held in genuine affection and respect by many of Llanbradach's early residents. One of her last acts was to give £1,000 towards the building of the Workmen's Hall. The church was closed as unsafe, and demolished in 1994.'

So I hope that this emphasises the inextricable link between Llanbradach, Llwyn Madoc and Pencerrig, and that it has given you the incentive to find out more about Miss Thomas and her family in general, and Pencerrig in particular. There will be a great deal more of her later in chapter 6, but let us now turn to the history of Pencerrig and the families who lived there.

Chapter 2

PENCERRIG

One story says that the original house at Pencerrig was somewhere near the Home Farm; another places it 'right up in the corner', and certainly there is evidence that some kind of building was tucked up into the corner by the green gate. The old stone road here is some ten feet about the level of the floor. That road must be well over a thousand years old, and the old house was built into the stone. Houses in those days were often knocked down and the stones and timber re-used over the years. The date of the original house remains uncertain.

Pencerrig, 1970

The black and white photograph on the previous page shows the magnificent chimneys that you would have seen as you came up the drive nearly 300 years ago. The original gabled end on the left was turned into staff quarters in 1970.

(Due to serous neglect this house is now a Building at Risk on the SAVE Britain's Heritage website, which is a very great shame.)

Over a century later the major extension was built by Mrs. Thomas (also Clara) when she moved in, around 1840. On the ground floor were two impressive reception rooms, and above them she built four large and gracious bedrooms. She would not have wanted to use the same stairs as the servants, so the unique flying staircase went up through the old outer wall to her bedroom. I believe that 'our' Clara stood on those stairs and led the servants below in prayer when she lived there.

So it has been a much altered seventeenth century house and it is notable as a good example of a medium-sized mid Wales estate, and was once home to one of Wales' foremost landscape painters, Thomas Jones, who was a student of the Picturesque, of whom you will read more later.

In those days people were used to food that was only half hot; the gentry accepted that their food had to come a long way from the kitchens, and Pencerrig was no exception. I know this because my late husband Mervyn wrote this when he was giving a Talk to the Probus Club in Llandrindod in 1997:

'I well remember my elder brother Patrick and I staying quite often at Pencerrig after we had come back from Canada in 1933. Two horrid small boys. We used to sleep up in the attic. Little did we know then that the rooms up there were full of Thomas Jones paintings, which were later to become so popular.

'A vivid memory I have of that period was of bombing the butler. I wonder *if any of you remember dear Mrs Warre who more recently lived in the lodge at Pencerrig? Well, it was her husband who, poor man, used to have to walk from the kitchens at the back of the house across the hall with the food to the dining room. It was before the top floor was burnt down, and now there are of course stringent fire restrictions; but then it was a perfect place for some very skilled high level bombing! I am sightly ashamed to say that we used to have great fun dropping things down on the poor man'.*

I smile at this because Mervyn became quite a well behaved man in later years, as some of you may remember him. But I think after eight years of wonderful freedom on Vancouver Island they were full of harmless fun and high jinks! Sadly the brother referred to was killed in WW II aged 23, and was the heir to Llwyn Madoc. So if he had lived Mervyn would not have inherited it, and I would not be sitting here writing about The Family.

THE HOUSE AT THE TOP OF THE ROCKS
by R C B Oliver

THE SETTING

'The banks of the parish of Llanelwedd ascend rapidly from the river Wye, and are crowned with rocky summits torn asunder and convulsed by some violent concussion of nature. Huge rocks jumbled together in various directions and, assuming a conical form, seem to have been disgorged from the bowels of the earth by the operations of volcanoes.' The Rev. Jonathan Williams, in the years just before 1820, thus described the setting of The House at the top of the Rocks in his History of Radnorshire.

Half a century earlier, Sir Thomas Cullum and his son, on a tour of Wales, described the seven miles from Builth to Llandrindod Wells in these words: 'The first part of the road is an ascent up a steep rocky mountain, then through an enclosed wooded country till you come to a large heath.'

Sir Thomas would not now recognise the old road from Builth to Llandrindod, between Llanelwedd and Wye Cottage, when it used to run close to the foot of the older quarries, past Tan-y-graig, which gave an average gradient of 1 in 20. It is not surprising that the squires of Llanelwedd Hall, Wellfield (Cefndyrys), and Pencerrig, in 1818-1820 had a new road built which is longer but less steep; the expense being repaid partly by tolls at the turnpike in Llanelwedd, and partly by increased rents paid by their tenant farmers.

A modern geologist would describe the Pencerrig area as 'an ideal site for the study of volcanic activity, with the shales lining the smooth, grassy hollows, with the harder bun-shaped dolerites forming conspicuous hummocks and ridges.'

A new drive to Pencerrig was laid down leading from the main road around the back of the house to the old farmyard past the kennels, with a protecting stone wall on the south side with flower beds and lawns. The great geologist Murchison, describing this locality in 1839, writes of the new approach to the house of Pencerrig, and his words leave no doubt that it is the more southerly of the two present drives, though a lodge was not built there till 1927.

Views were there to be enhanced by man in the 18th century, and generally included a lake. If one did not exist it was created. In 1796 Thomas Jones' daybook records a payment for making a reservoir in the new garden. The stream on the north side was dammed, which flooded the main road from Builth to Llandrindod. Not deterred by this setback, the road had to be moved. In 1795 the Great Pool silted up and the mud had to be cleared at further expense. When complete, the six acre lake was held to be a great improvement to the view.

THE GARDEN

The garden was relatively small, covering about an acre. It was dominated by a large circular lawn to the south of the house; this was bordered on the south by a raised earth bank against a high stone wall which encloses the garden.

Thomas Jones' diaries record that by 1794/95 there was an old and a new garden, the latter being created by himself. It is unclear whether these are refences only to the productive garden, because Jones planted the new garden with a variety of fruit trees, including pears from Maesllwch (which is still well cared for in its majestic setting above Glasbury by the de Winton family).

The site of the new garden is not clear, but the field below the drive to the south of the house is recorded as an orchard on the tithe of 1845.

The kitchen garden was about 250 yards south east of the house, which was typical in those days as of course there were plenty of gardeners to bring in the produce each day, so there was no need for the garden to be near the house.

Of course this is all in the past as the whole place is now sadly in a terrible state of repair but could be brought back into shape under a careful hand.

FORESTRY

The constant use of timber for building, fuel, furniture and ships, as well as deforestation to create farmland have, over the centuries, denuded Radnorshire of much of its fine, slow-growing oak forests, but the frequency of the Welsh words 'coed (wood); llwyn (grove); and derw' (oak) shows how well wooded Pencerrig's valley sides once were. Coed Mawr (Great Wood) must once have been one of the chief glories of the view from Pencerrig to the Carneddau Hills, says James Baker in his Picturesque Guide to the Local Beauties of Wales (1794), and this is borne out by another quote which compares the *'enormous gloom of the unwooded wastes of Radnor Forest with the cultivated and wooded valleys of Pencerrig'.*

When he was the guest of Thomas Jones the Artist (1742-1803), Baker also wrote, *'There are no estates in all these parts where the native*

*oak groves are more carefully preserved than on Pencerrig which, blending with
the majestic rocks and romantic hills abounding thereon, form great characters
of beauty and delight. A comely height that rises about Pencerrig, latterly
covered with a grove of large oaks, was felled by the last possessor of the estates.'*

With a fine oak fetching in the 18th century as much as £9, timber
was a tempting source of easy income, and Major John Jones who
inherited Pencerrig in 1782, (although he lived there from 1750,
until his death in 1787), seems to have felled a lot of the older trees.
But from entries in the daybook he kept from 1788-1797 we know
that Thomas Jones, the next owner, more than replaced what his
brother had felled. There is a memo for April 1793 to the effect that
325 young oak trees had been transplanted out of the two nurseries
into the ground enclosed for them, and 300 or thereabouts, last
year into the Great Wood. Conifers too were planted, including
some larch, which were a novelty at this time, and doubtless Scots

Scene from Pencerrig by Thomas Jones

pine which was popular since the Civil War of 1642-1652, when the Radnor gentry planted them as a sign of Stuart affections, and were still known locally as 'Charlie Trees'.

The oak timber from Pencerrig was said to have been used for the keel of the famous but ill-fated warship, the Royal George, launched in 1756, and lost off Portsmouth in 1782.

There was an old staircase at Llwyn Madoc when I first went there which was always referred to as the Royal George. I think it must have been made from the timbers thereof.

When Pencerrig was sold in 1958, the Forestry Commission took a long lease on some 130 acres which were planted with conifers.

Chapter 3

THE FAMILIES OF PENCERRIG 1500s-1838

From the departure of the Romans until the Battle of Bosworth, which in 1485 brought to an end the Wars of the Roses and put Henry Tudor on the English throne, Wales had enjoyed no long period free from warfare. However, in the next two centuries, and especially after the 1542 Act of Union, Wales was comparatively peaceful, and this gave many of the old Welsh families the chance to build up their estates by hard work, careful marriages, and by selling their surplus livestock, wool and timber to English buyers; while many younger sons won fortunes in careers at Court, in the Judiciary and the Church, and from success in the higher ranks of Commerce and Trade.

THE POWELL FAMILY 1602-1684

One such family owned and lived at Pencerrig from its earliest recorded history: the ap Howell (Powell) family who claimed Elystan Glodrydd as their progenitor, and who can be clearly traced back to Elizabethan times. From this family may have come Dafydd ap Howell of Diserth who was among other things a lawyer – a profession made more lucrative by great changes in the laws and the substitution of English for Welsh in legal documents after the Act of Union. He lived in the first half of the 16th century.

Of the same family was Thomas Powell (c. 1572-1635), also a lawyer, but now remembered more for his pioneer work on public records, which he wrote after being Attorney General in the Marches of Wales from 1613 to 1622. The will dated 1585 of John Lloyd of Towy, squire to Queen Elizabeth I and Steward of the Manor of

Builth, in which church he lies buried, mentions a debt due to the testator by David Powell of Llanelwedd.

As early as 1602 the Powell family were rich enough for Sibilla, daughter of Thomas ap Howell, to have wed Thomas Vaughan of Llowes, son of Roger Vaughan of Clyro, who was M.P. for Radnorshire from 1572 to 1583, and High Sheriff in 1580. Later, the Powells intermarried with the well-known Gwynnes of Glanbran, near Cynghordy in Carmarthenshire, of which only a ruin is left after a massive fire.

The family continued to prosper, and their property spread south in Llanelwedd and north in Diserth as we learn from the Presentments at the Court Baron of 1623 for the Manor of Elfael, when Thomas Powell, gent., appears fourth on the list of inhabitants of the township of Diserth and second on the list for Llanelwedd; and in the Rent Rolls of the Lordship of Colwyn (c. 1670-1680) Thomas Powell, gent., appears in both these parishes, in the case of Diserth for Tyn-y-coed Mawr.

That Pencerrig was occupied by this family in the 17th century is proved by the signature of Thomas Powell of Llanelwedd, gent. and the date January 1631, on one of the documents in the Pencerrig Collection deposited in the National Library of Wales in 1953. However, the family fortunes had declined in 1684 partly through the cost of the Civil War (1642-1652); partly keeping up with the Gwynnes of Llanelwedd Hall; providing marriage portions for their daughters; and finally through the lack of male heirs, which sadly would plague Pencerrig in later years.

THE GRIFFITHS and THE SCOURFIELDS 1684-1730

The mortgage had been given in 1684 by Mr. Thomas Powell to Mr James Donne. The property was inherited by his son, subject to the mortgage. As he had no legal heirs it was passed to his three sisters subject to the mortgage; they were Mary the wife of Jeremiah

Griffiths, Ann the wife of Walter Williams, and the unmarried Sibilla Powell.

In 1697 Walter and Ann Williams and Sibilla sold their share to Jeremiah Griffiths, who died in or about 1712, and upon his death his widow, Mary, succeeded to the property for life, with remainder to their son, also Jeremiah. But in 1720, Mr. and Mrs. Scourfield, who had become entitled to Donne's mortgage, foreclosed the property, and in April 1730 they sold it to **Mr. John Hope** of Lincoln's Inn, the only son of Middleton Hope of Llandrindod Wells. He never married, so the estate was inherited by his niece, **Hannah.**

Mary Griffiths, who was widowed in 1718, may have stayed on as a tenant, but the house could have seen little of her son Jeremiah, because after being a scholar at Christ College, Brecon, he went to University to take his Arts degree, and from 1684 he was a Master at the Lady Hawkins Free Grammar School at Kington. By 1694 he must, like his father, have qualified for the Church, because in that year he was not only a Master at Christ College, where he had the reputation of being a fine mathematician and astronomer, but had already held the living of Diserth for 8 years. In fact he was, before 1698, compelled by Bishop Watson of St. David's to reside in one or other of his livings, which we learn from the Ecclesiastical Visitations Returns of 1733, were Diserth, Bettws Diserth, and Llandrindod where he then lived, holding a service every morning.

The James Donne of the mortgage was one of a wealthy, widespread family of the Llansantffraid yn Elfael area of Radnorshire. He married Susannah Watkins, whose family were originally of Hay; she inherited Tregoyd, and their daughter married a Devereux, of the family which had produced as early as 1549 the Viscounts of Hereford.

William Scourfield of the mortgage was the eldest son of a noted Pembrokeshire family whose seat was Moat, in the parish of New Moat, in the hundred of Dau Gleddau. He was a student at Lincoln's Inn, where he may have met John Hope. He married Anne, heiress of

William Phillips, Barrister-at-Law, Recorder and Mayor of Brecon, whom Hugh Thomas, Deputy Herald for Wales, described in 1698 as '*of great fortune, rank and quality*', and whose father-in-law, John Walters, was one of the two wealthiest men in Brecon.

In 1731 Scourfield became High Sheriff of Breconshire. He and his wife may well have used Pencerrig as a summer home, though there is no factual evidence of this.

THE HOPES 1730-1761

John Hope seems to have spent most of his life in London, where he practised at Lincoln's Inn. As already mentioned, he was the only son of Middleton Hope of Llandrindod Hall, (which later became the Grosvenor Hotel); his mother was a Miss Middleton of Chirk Castle, and whose father, John Hope, belonged to the Hope family of Denbighshire and Flintshire.

John's mother was a Miss Birch of Garnstone, near Weobley, in Herefordshire, and a niece to John Birch, the Parliamentarian Colonel in the Civil War, who enriched his whole family by speculating in Church lands; but of whom it was said, '*His Presbyterian principles were even dearer to him than his own advancement.*'

John Hope's three sisters had by 1716 all wed and left their home at Llandrindod Hall, to which Thomas Jones in his Memoirs refers to in about 1746, as 'the old deserted mansion of my maternal great grandfather.'

THE JONES FAMILY 1761-1807 and the LINK WITH TREFONNEN

The Jones family of Trefonnen were by origin of Llwynygath and Erwddalen in the parish of Llanfihangel Brynpabuan in north Breconshire, where Elystan Glodrydd himself is said to have had a residence. The elder son, David Jones of Erwddalen was a drover, and went to London where he had made money enough in silk weaving, and soldiering in the Parliamentary army; so he returned to Wales a wealthy man in about 1660.

He was clearly a man of substance and very well thought of, 'and after some years he sold his Breconshire patrimony and bought Trefonnen and some other tenements nearby', including Llwyn y Gog or Bach y Graig Isaf, which later became the Pump House in Llandrindod Wells. His second wife was Jane Powell of Llwyn Cwta, Nantmel, by whom he had a daughter and two sons.

The younger son, Thomas, had been educated at an Academy of Dissenting Ministry in Shrewsbury. In 1713 he married Elizabeth, the eldest daughter of Middleton Hope of Llandrindod Hall and sister of John Hope, mentioned above. Elizabeth probably owned Garn Fawr farm in Bettws Diserth where the local Dissenters were accustomed to meet. From there he went on to minister at a chapel in Tetbury Gloucestershire, building a meeting house there at his own expense in 1710.

Returning to Trefonnen every year, in 1715 he built Caebach

Trefonnen

chapel near his home, and it was commonly known then as 'Mr. Jones' Meeting House'.

It was upon their only surviving daughter, **Hannah**, that the Pencerrig estate was devolved on the death of her uncle John Hope, who had bought the Pencerrig estate from the Scourfields in 1730. He belonged to the Trefonnen branch of the family of which The Congregational 250th Commemorative Volume of 1912 said that, *'They were men of high standing, and some of the chief landowners of the locality descended from them, having inherited their wealth and denied their principles.* Many of the chief landowners of the locality were descended from them.

Hannah married her first cousin, Thomas Jones (1711-1782), the son of her father's elder brother John (and father of Thomas the artist), of Trefonnen at St. Mary's Church, Gloucester in 1738, when she was only seventeen. This union thus joined two branches of a powerful family in the small circle of Radnorshire landowners. Both had strong traditions of Dissent. Incidentally the coat of arms of the Joneses of Trefonnen bears the symbol of Elystan Glodrydd, the Welsh prince, the progenitor also of the Powells who built Pencerrig originally.

When the newly married couple took up residence at Trefonnen in 1738, Llandrindod was on the brink of discovery by the rich and idle spongers who had flocked to the Spas of that time. So the town now, after a century as a little known watering-place, suddenly attracted an influx of bright and dissolute visitors. Trefonnen was surrounded by worldly bustle and unseemly activities. By 1750 Thomas and Hannah had a thriving young family of six children, and the changed atmosphere of Llandrindod was not to their strictly dissenting tastes. So with the family and the servants they moved to peaceful Pencerrig, which was much quieter and suited them better. It was there that the rest of their 16 children were born, though only 9 survived to adult years, three dying in the small-pox outbreak of 1766.

Two of the three watering places of the 'healing waters' sprang to the surface on land owned by the Joneses since 1660, when the same family had bought Trefonnen and the Pump House.

Thomas and Hannah leased Trefonnen to a Mr. Grosvenor of Shrewsbury, who was already the tenant at Llandrindod Hall but it was not used a great deal, since the Middleton Hope children had grown up and left home for marriage or a career. Mr. Grosvenor had converted the Hall into a large and luxurious hotel, well described in Pritchard's Llandrindod Guide of 1825.

CAEBACH CHAPEL

John Hope had died without issue in 1761 in London, then with the death of Hannah, the family connection and the Methodist connection at Caebach came to an end, although many of their large number of children are buried in the family vault here, including Thomas Jones the artist. Despite this however, Caebach continued, the ministry being supported by Hannah's Carreguan legacy.

Caebach Chapel

Who would have thought that when this quiet congregational chapel was first built, that it would become a veritable hotbed of Methodist activity during the eighteenth century? It was visited over many years by Howell Harris who preached there many times. He stayed often at Trefonnen, and in later years, when the family moved there, also became a visitor at Pencerrig.

Caebach retains a substantial

amount of its fabric of 1715, and has most unusually, a family burial vault which houses the remains of its founding family, the Jones' of Trefonnen. In 1804 it was remodelled and again in 1840, which included the construction of its high box pews which face a gabled-end pulpit. It is also notable for its 1804 ogee windows: an arch shape with two curved sides meeting at the apex.

[Incidentally the neighbouring church, St. Cewydd, Diserth, close to Pencerrig, also has ancient box pews that the local gentry owned.]

It is heart warming to learn that upon the chapel's closure in 2019, Addoldai, the Welsh Religious Buildings Trust acquired the chapel the following year from the United Reformed Church on a 25 year lease. Addoldai is a charity established to take into ownership or care a selection of redundant chapels that are historically and/ or architecturally significant to the story of chapel building and Nonconformity in Wales.

I have very much enjoyed trying to collate a huge amount of material from so many different sources, and it would be far too long to include all that I have read. For this reason I have put in a great deal more at the end (in Part 2) because I have found it so very interesting to learn what a large part some of these courageous men played in the birth of the remarkable Methodist Revival in the 18th century. There is plenty more online for anyone interested, but I have managed to avoid using it.

TREFECCA FAWR

Trefecca Fawr has played quite a large part in my life over the years. When I was first married and came to live in Wales we used to visit David Gwynne's widow Madge when she lived there, as the Gwynnes had done for many generations. They were kinsmen of my late husband, and their son Teddy and his wife Judy were great friends of ours. Very sadly Teddy died in his early fifties; they had two daughters, Sarah and Eliza.

Much later some other good friends of mine bought Trefecca Fawr where they entertained lavishly from the mid nineties for about twenty years, and many well known Christian speakers came and led meetings and spoke on many occasions. I think we all longed for and even expected Revival to start right there again. Literally thousands had gathered in the surrounding fields, two centuries before, to listen to William Williams, Howell Harris and Daniel Rowlands, who were the giants of the Methodist Revival.

We had wonderful times there, but sadly no Revival.

Since writing about these astonishing men and women I have at last begun to understand the difference between the Dissenters which the afore mentioned were. They actually rebelled against the established church and were very greatly persecuted in this country, so we must realise how courageous they were. Many others went to America where they had more freedom.

The Reformation of course changed this in the UK, and the Act of Toleration in 1689 made things a great deal easier for the Dissenters, who were then allowed to meet in small numbers: hence the emergence of House groups.

HOWELL HARRIS (1714-1775)

At the time of Howell Harris, Wales was still relatively isolated from England. Despite the Acts of Union under Henry VIII, the Welsh still preserved distinct cultural and historical traditions. It was physically remote from England in that her roads were hazardous, so people tended to think twice before they visited Wales. The use of the Welsh language was another isolating factor. Griffith Jones wrote, *'There are some advantages peculiar to the Welsh tongue favourable to religion, as being perhaps the chastest in Europe. Its books and writings are free from the infection and deadly venom of Atheism, Deism, Infidelity, Arianism, Popery, lewd plays, immodest romances, and love intrigues; which poison minds, captivate all the senses, and prejudice so many.'*

This could perhaps have been a major reason why the Holy Spirit was so easily received in Wales during the coming decades.

Harris was born at Trefecca, in Brecon in 1714. He was a school-master at Llangorse for three years, until 1735. He liked to record how sinful he was as a boy, but he then discovered that God loves sinners who truly repent, and he found that he could not do it in his own strength. After a great struggle he wrote *'I chose the Lord for my portion. I believe I was then effectually called to be a follower of the Lamb.'* In May 1735 he was filled with the Holy Spirit when he was listening to his vicar, the Revd. Pryce Davies in Llangasty church, who was talking about receiving the Sacrament, *'if you are not fit to come to the Lord's Table, you are not fit to live, nor fit to die.'*

Painting of Trefecca College by Marcia Gibson-Watt

On Whit Sunday he realised that he had been accepted by God, then on June 18th he experienced a manifestation of God's presence. *'Being in secret prayer, I felt suddenly my heart melting within me like wax before the fire with love to God my Saviour; and also felt not only love, peace etc., but longing to be dissolved, and to be with Christ. Then was a cry in my inmost soul, which I was totally unacquainted with before, Abba, Father! Abba, Father! I could not help calling God my Father; I knew that I was His child; and that He loved me and heard me. My soul being filled and satiated, crying, Tis enough, I am satisfied. Give me strength and I will follow Thee through fire and water.'*

Harris was *not a great preacher like Rowland*, but his presence was commanding and he was probably the most successful evangelist that Wales has ever known.

Chapter 4

THOMAS JONES (The Artist) 1742-1803

Thomas' mother, Hannah Jones, outlived her husband, but she stayed on at Pencerrig, running the mansion for her eldest son, John, who remained a bachelor. He died two years before his mother who, in her bereavement, took comfort and solace in the little chapel at Caebach. It still stands just off the road from Llandrindod Wells to Llanyre, the remarkable Memorial for the Jones family is still to be seen on the West wall. The stable (for the Minister's horse) is still there – just opposite.

As we have already seen it had been built in 1720 by Hannah's father, the Rev. Thomas Jones of Tefonnen and Tetbury, and was commonly known then as 'Mr. Jones' Meeting House'

The interior of Cae Bach Chapel

It is through the kindness of Canon J. H. Adams of St. Agnes, Cornwall, and his collection of books, letters, documents and pictures that it has been possible to piece together the domestic life of Thomas Jones in Naples.

Thomas was destined for the church, but was determined to paint, and like his fellow artists longed to travel to Italy, the cultural centre of Europe; however parental consent had to be won, so to this end he spent a year at Pencerrig from September 1755. He put this year to good use, as he said: *'painting and drawing enough pictures to clear all financial demands, and leave a few guineas in my pocket'.*

Pictures of the famous Oak Trees at Pencerrig
which Thomas Jones enjoyed painting so much.

He spent a year at William Shipley's Drawing School, before becoming a pupil of Richard Wilson from 1761 for two years, training in classical landscape painting.

He spent the years from 1776 to 1783 in Italy, studying art. After two years work and study on his own in Rome, he moved to Naples. His oil sketches from this period were undoubtedly ahead of his time, using, as an example, 'The Wall in Naples' 1782 (oil on paper laid down on board, National Gallery, London.)

In Italy he met a widow, Maria Monck, who was born Maria Turnstaat of Copenhagen in 1745. She had come to live there, and had been received into the Roman Catholic Church, and married in 1777, only to lose her husband shortly afterwards.

Thomas and Maria lived together in a modest house, from about 1779, but Thomas had his qualms, and confessed that 'for family reasons I did not think it prudent to own to the connection.' Two daughters, Anna Maria and Elizabetta, were born to the couple, in all probability out of wedlock. So Thomas seems to have tried to keep his liaison secret, but when he returned with his family to London in 1783, the position had to be regularised.

After the death of his father in 1782 Thomas returned to live in England with his family. The couple, still unmarried, settled happily in London. This must have caused a great deal of pain to his mother, who came to London and stayed there for a year, during which Thomas and Maria were married in the Protestant Church. Respectability had been donned, but by the harsh law of the time the two little girls were not legitimised, and this was later to cause much legal trouble.

What a travesty looking back on this: it is hard now to realise how enormous was the stigma of illegitimacy in those days.

His brother John's early death in 1787, aged only 48, meant that Thomas was now head of the family and therefore heir to Pencerrig, which must have been quite a shock.

Thomas finally returned to Wales late in 1789 via Brecon, where his mother had died a month earlier at the home of her other son, Frederick, on her way home. She was buried in Caebach where so much had happened in the Dissenting years.

Thomas never caught the fervour of the Methodist Revival which his parents had embraced so wholeheartedly, and had spread rapidly in and around Caebach Chapel, with Howell Harris preaching there on many occasions.

As a landscape artist, Jones was taught in the Romantic tradition, inspired by Richard Wilson, who was born near Machynlleth in Powys and loved the mountainous landscape that he painted so often. Like so many artists Thomas Jones was never truly acclaimed during his lifetime, but he is now very well known in art circles for being way ahead of his time by painting en plein air, which was hitherto unknown. This new method signalled a significant advance in landscape art.

The Wall in Naples

This small study is beautifully calculated with near-abstract placing of the elements in the composition; a sensitive observation of all the marks; scaffolding holes; wear of the wall; but then the brilliant strip above the wall of a beige colour (perhaps of another building) and then the intense blue of the Italian sky. It is quite remarkable that this was all a foretaste of what Matisse and others were to achieve a century later.

Pages from the sketchbook of Thomas Jones

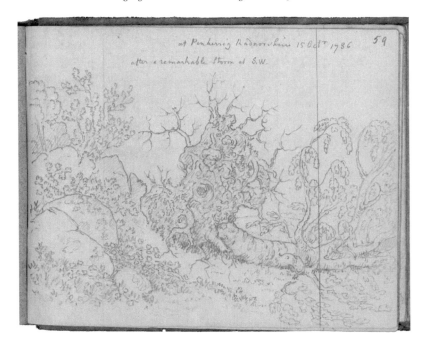

Thomas Jones was a master of plein air, observation and sketching in oil. The apparent modernity of such a work was clearly fascinating to scholars when his work eventually came on the market. He has a freshness of colouring and a unity and immediacy of feeling that arise from sketches being painted in the open. He thus emerges as an artist with extraordinary vision, worthy of the term 'Great Welsh Artist' with his place in a European tradition.

For at least 150 years after Thomas' death all his remaining pictures were owned by the family. As soon as they began to be sold at auction in 1952 they reached unexpectedly high prices; the scholars in the important galleries of Swansea, London, Cardiff, Dublin, Manchester and the U.S.A immediately realised their great intellectual worth. Is it not astonishing to think of the enormous contribution Thomas Jones made in a simple and understated contribution to the story of art?

He spent the rest of his life at his beloved Pencerrig as a country squire, but it seems that Maria was never really accepted, so it must have been very lonely for her as the girls were educated in London and only returned to Pencerrig for the holidays.

Thomas, however, took an active interest in his estate, and did an immense amount to enhance it. He made new agricultural developments, and planted a great many interesting and varied trees, as well as developing the landscape and improving the garden. Much of these are faithfully recorded in his sketchbooks. He also made many improvements to the eighteenth century house. In 1791, he even wrote a poem entitled "Petraeia" about his love for Pencerrig. *(Pen is head and Cerrig is stone in Welsh.)*

He now only painted for his own amusement, and he entered into the life that was expected and enjoyed by wealthy landowners. He was a Magistrate, and High Sheriff of Radnorshire in 1791.

During these happy years he was visited by an Italian friend, Francesco Renaldi, who painted in 1797 the Conversation Piece, which is reproduced here, by permission of the National Museum of

Wales, where the original now hangs. It shows on the left 'Madam' Jones, as she was known locally, the two daughters at the hammer piano, and Thomas Jones at the easel. Some have named the man in the background as Captain John Dale, who later married the younger girl. It is more likely to be the Rev. David Jones, a younger brother of Thomas, and then a bachelor, who lived not far away at Gladestry; the sober clothes certainly suggest a cleric.

Furthermore, documents in the possession of Canon Adams show that Captain Dale was at sea for the whole of 1797 when the picture was painted, and there is evidence that he did not meet his future wife 'till about 1803, when he first visited Llandrindod Wells to take the waters. Captain Dale made a second marriage in 1812, and Canon Adams is a great-grandson of that marriage. This attractive painting, however, has tragic overtones, for Madam Jones was already suffering from the painful malady which killed her less than two years later.

Conversation Piece by Francesco Renaldi

Sad to say, Thomas died in 1803, and so he did not live to see his two girls married on the same day in April 1804 in Llanelwedd Church; his brother, the Rev. David, who performed the ceremonies, died in 1809.

Anna Maria, the older girl, born in 1780, married Thomas Thomas of Llanbradach, Glamorgan, but she died in 1807, followed by her only child, a boy, in 1810.

Elizabetta Francesca, the younger, born in 1781, wed Captain John Dale of the Honourable East India Company, but she lost her only child, a girl, in April 1806, and she herself died before the year was out at Clifton near Bristol, but was buried in Llandrindod.

Pencerrig still contained numerous reminders of Thomas Jones the Artist, including many of his paintings and sketch books. The drawings in some of the sketch books, even contain small details which can be readily recognised today, two hundred years after they were drawn.

Chapter 5

SOME OF THE DISSENTERS

THE LINK WITH LLANELWEDD HALL

The will of Thomas Jones had devised Pencerrig House and that part of the estate in Llanelwedd and Diserth to Anna Maria; these passed to her infant son on her death, and on his death to her widower, Thomas Thomas of Llanbradach.

To Elizabetta went the rest of the estate, mainly property in Cefnllys, Llandrindod and Llanbadan fawr, including Trefonnen and the Pump House which passed to her widower Captain John Dale on her death. However, he lost it, following a legitimacy lawsuit which was successfully contested in 1813 by Middleton Jones (Thomas the artist's brother and uncle to Elizabetta) who in turn devised the estate to his sister Elizabeth's son.

| Pause a moment to consider this: it seems horribly unfair.

THOMAS THOMAS

Thomas Thomas was devastated by the death of his wife Anna Maria; however he remarried in 1811, a year after the death of his only child. His new bride was Bridget Gwynne, the elder daughter of Marmaduke Gwynne, Esq. of nearby Llanelwedd Hall. She and her sister and two brothers, had been orphaned when the eldest of them was only ten years old. At twenty one, her eldest brother Marmaduke had eloped with and married Mary Meredith at Gretna Green, the elder daughter of a well-to-do Kington tradesman: a marriage which, after the birth of a daughter, ended in 1809.

Bridget doubtless hoped for a happier life at Pencerrig, but sadly her son, also called Thomas, born in 1812, lived only a year.

So it is through the second marriage of Thomas Thomas of Llwyn Madoc to Bridget Gwynne, that connects Llwyn Madoc to Llanelwedd Hall as well as neighbouring Pencerrig.

Enter MARMADUKE GWYNNE 1691-1769 *(a century late!)*

One of the reasons that I mention two Marmaduke Gwynnes here is because we as a family have a particular interest in Marmaduke's maternal grandfather, born in 1643. He was Second Judge on the Anglesey circuit and became a wealthy landowner. There is a very good portrait of him in his robes by the great Kneller. He died in 1708.

However it is his grandson, also Marmaduke, in whom we are even more interested because he returned from London to take up a substantial inheritance of Garth and Llanelwedd in 1708 in his late teens. He became a magistrate, and was High Sheriff of Radnorshire in 1718. He was my husband's fifth generation grandfather.

So he not only provides the connection between Garth House and Llwyn Madoc, but also a link between those two mansions with Pencerrig and Llanelwedd Hall. I feel the latter is perhaps especially significant because the remaining kitchen wing of the old house which was burned down in 1955 is now the offices on the Royal Welsh Showground.

Marmaduke lived at Garth House, near Builth Wells, and was converted to Methodism by Howell Harris, and served as a legal adviser and financial supporter to the Methodists. He played a pivotal role in the 1769 Revival, of which there is a great deal more about him in Part Two.

Charles and John Wesley first visited Garth in 1747. The story goes that Charles stayed here to recuperate after becoming ill with pneumonia on his way back from Ireland. Marmaduke's daughter Sarah Gwynne (known as Sally) nursed him, and it was love at first sight. They were married in April 1749 and John (Wesley) officiated at the little church called Llanlleonfel, only half a mile across the fields from Garth House. Apparently it was a sombre affair with much prayer and hymn singing. They had nine children, but sadly only three of them reached adulthood. The youngest, Sarah, was born in 1726, and it was a long and happy marriage, unusually for the Wesley family it seems.

The Wesleyan Society used to visit Garth House and Llanleonfel church every year until the early 2000s.

When I first came to live in Wales in 1961, long before the M4 was built, it was considered very remote. I remember reading a biography of John Wesley, and could not believe how many miles he managed to travel on horseback: to and from London to Wales and other far away places, covering thousands of laborious miles which must have taken months at a time. The route was very rough, and would often be beset by highwayman which made it dangerous to say the least. It is hard to imagine this in these latter days of instant gratification, and when people get mildly hysterical if they cannot contact someone immediately through social media. There was no telephone then, of course, let alone a mobile, nor WhatsApp until nearly three generations later.

On this subject I found a reference to a certain Lorenzo Kirkpatrick Hall, Esq. of Pencerrig, in 1863, with an entry in an old diary found at Brynwern, Newbridge-on-Wye (later a part of the Llysdinam estate), which refers to a code of signals used from Llysdinam to the Summer House at Pencerrig by Edward Hall and Henry Venables in 1863.

What an ingenious way to communicate before all the modern technology took over. I love to think of this as I drive along the fast stretch of road between Newbridge and Builth!

A NOTE ON THE DEATH OF
HANNAH JONES OF PENCERRIG

Hannah Jones died on 19 November, 1789, at the Brecon home of her son Frederick, but was buried in Caebach Chapel. A month later a remarkable sermon was preached at Caebach by the Rev. John Thomas, who was a former minister at Caebach, occasioned by the death of Madam Jones of Pencerrig. It made such an impression that in 1791 it was printed on the private press at Trefecca, the birthplace and later the site of a religious settlement founded by Howell Harris, the great revivalist, whom Hannah Jones and her husband so constantly befriended during his early, dangerous missions in Radnorshire.

John Thomas was born in 1730 in Myddfai, Carmarthenshire, of *thrift-less* parents, and brought up largely by relatives. After conversion by Howell Harris, he worked for a time as a servant in the house of Griffith Jones of *Llanddowror* before entering the Dissenters' Academy at Abergavenny in 1761. He was ordained in 1767 as minister of Rhayader, Caebach and Garn (Bettws Diserth), in which he ministered until 1778. He then preached privately in different parts of Radnorshire until 1794, when he returned to his native county. The year and place of his death are not known with certainty.

In his autobiography Rhad Ras (Free Grace), published in 1810, Thomas refers to the sermon he preached at Caebach on Philippians 1: verse 21: '*For me to live is Christ and to die is gain*', adding that '*Religion and preaching have come to an end after the death of these two (i.e. Mr. and Mrs. Jones of Pencerrig); there is no sign of religion in any of their progeny up to now,*' wrote R.C.B. Oliver.

In the sermon itself, after referring to the Christian life of the parents, he addressed himself directly to the offspring and in no uncertain terms compared the mode of living of some of them very unfavourably with that of their parents.

This public admonition so incensed the son Middleton Jones, Esq., attorney, of Penybont Court, that he soon deprived John Thomas of the house and Caebach of the Manse and attached fields that Hannah had given them: an action which may explain the omission of Middleton's name from the family memorial in the Chapel.

DISSENT

It is interesting to note that the Middletons and Birches held dissenting views, which seem to have been passed on by Mrs. Middleton Hope (née Birch) to her three daughters, who all married into dissenting families. Mary, the youngest, married in 1716 John Jones of Cribarth in North Breconshire, and their eldest daughter, Anne, married Evan Thomas of Llwyn Madoc as his second wife. Just to re-cap, Elizabeth married the Revd. Thomas Jones of Trefonnen, the Dissenting Minister at Tetbury who built Caebach chapel. They were the parents of the committed Hannah.

Evan Thomas built Llwyn Madoc in 1747 and he married Elizabeth Walters, daughter of an eminent and well-to-do non-conformist minister at Rhayader; she was the mother of Henry who succeeded

Portraits of Evan Thomas and Elizabeth Walters

Portrait of Anne Jones of Cribarth,
Evan's second wife

him, and after Elizabeth died, he married Anne Jones of Cribarth in 1760, but she died soon after.

Cribarth later went to the Pencerrig Joneses. This Cribarth family was indissolubly associated with the Nonconformist chapel built in 1714 at nearby Troedrhiwdalar, though there was an earlier chapel on a field of Cribarth itself late in the 17th century. Of David Jones of Cribarth and his brother John of Cwmcammarch, the Congregational 250th Commemorative Volume of 1912 says, *'They were men of high standing, and some of the chief* landowners of the locality descended from them, having inherited their wealth and denied their principles'.

Picture of Cribarth by Marcia Gibson-Watt

We learn from his diaries that Howell Harris was a welcome guest at Trefonnen, and he surely preached many times at Caebach chapel, which Hannah had helped to endow with the freehold of Carreguan Farm in Llansantffraed yn Elfael. Even when living at Pencerrig seven miles away, she and her family continued to worship there each Sunday morning. There too, a large number of the family were interred, and a remarkable family wall Memorial erected. *'After her death in 1789', says the History of Nonconformist Chapels in Wales, 'Nonconformity lost its hold on this family;'* but not all members of the family were Dissenters.

Chapter 6

MISS CLARA THOMAS

Now at last we can learn more about the significant link between Pencerrig and Llwyn Madoc that was mentioned at the very beginning. I hope you will perceive the significance of Miss Thomas, and how she came to be the central figure of the Pencerrig story.

Her father Henry Thomas, of Llwyn Madoc, whose family, like that of the Joneses of Trefonnen, claimed descent from Elystan Glodrydd, married Clara (daughter of Thomas Thomas of Llanbradach) in September 1835 at Bathwich, an elegant suburb of Bath. Just in case you are completely muddled, his first wife was Anna Maria Jones, the eldest daughter of Thomas Jones the Artist.

Portrait of Thomas Thomas   *Mrs. Clara Thomas (senior) with her children Evan and Clara*

2

Though Mr. and Mrs. Henry Thomas made improvements at Pencerrig, they seem to have lived mainly at Llwyn Madoc; they rented out Pencerrig, which had failed to produce a male heir since 1787 when Thomas Jones succeeded to the estate, and this marriage of the two Thomas families was not much more fortunate. The first son born to Clara and Henry Thomas in 1837 at Castle House, Brecon, who was christened Evan Thomas Gwynne died, aged 14 months, at Tenby, where there is in St. Mary's Church a tablet to his memory. Inscribed in Latin which translates, *'In affectionate remembrance of the dearly beloved first born infant son of Henry Thomas of Llwyn Madoc, in Siluria, and of his wife Clara. Born 16th October 1837 in Brecon. Died 4th December here.'* It ends with a touching *quatrain* expressing the parents' great grief. A baby girl had also died in infancy.

In happier times another son, Evan Llewelyn, was born in 1839, and in 1842 a daughter, also named Clara. We shall now return to this remarkable lady as there is so much more to learn about her.

Henry Thomas of Llwyn Madoc, Pencerrig, and Llanbradach died in 1863, in which year he was High Sheriff of Breconshire, but his heir, Evan, only enjoyed his very rich inheritance for a few months, for he died tragically in Paris the following year, at the age of 25. This suddenly left his sister, 'our' Clara, one of the wealthiest women in Wales. She had already inherited Llanbradach from her father in 1863, and now only a year later, devastated by the tragic loss of her elder brother so suddenly and, at the very early age of 22 she inherited Llwyn Madoc and Pencerrig from her mother's side of the family.

This was of course a huge responsibility for a young woman, but she embraced the challenge with a remarkable sense of duty, generosity and unstinting beneficence for the rest of her life. Happily she got on very well with her mother and had her guiding hand for the first 13 years after her father's death.

HER FRIENDS

Miss Thomas had two close companions. One was Rosalind Phillimore, daughter of E. G. B. Phillimore, the famous Celtic scholar and editor of Y Cymmrodorion from 1889 to 1891. This is a London-based Welsh learned society, with membership open to all. It was first established in 1751 as a social, cultural, literary, and philanthropic institution. Perhaps it is not so well known that Miss Thomas was sufficiently interested in things Welsh to join this Honourable Society of Cymmrodorion in 1887.

Edwin Davies of Brecon in his preface to the 1905 edition of the History of Radnorshire thanks Miss Thomas (with others) for help given in facilitating the progress of the edition through its various stages.

Her other great friend was Gertrude Lewis Lloyd, one of the daughters of Thomas Lewis Lloyd of Nantgwillt, which famously was the house that was submerged when they flooded the Elan valley. It was known as the 'House under the Water' in the television play of that name . It had been submerged when Elan Valley was flooded in 1901.

The two young ladies must have been extremely intrepid because they used to visit each other by crossing the wild and deserted area of very rough ground between the Elan Valley and Llwyn Madoc. It would have taken a measure of courage. They used to travel in a pony-drawn gambo which I imagine was extremely uncomfortable to say the least. I have ridden this route on a horse several times, but only in good weather and I was always very wary of the bogs, especially Carnau which used to be a challenge for horses. Maybe the hill was not quite so wet in those days.

Gertrude must have been a great solace to Miss Thomas after her mother died in 1877. She helped in her church, educational and charitable work, and she always shared with her the Sunday School classes for boys and girls at Llwyn Madoc. She also took her turn at conducting Morning and Evening prayers: Miss Thomas was clearly very devout, and I love the reference (in South Wales Squires) of old Mr. Pearce the butler, coming into the drawing room to announce solemnly that *"Prayers is ready, M'm"*.

My mother-in law used to tell me this, as she actually remembered him saying this when she was a young girl.

There was always a bedroom kept ready for Gertrude at Llwyn Madoc. She died in 1907, and was buried in Eglwys Oen Duw church, where there is a stained glass window to her memory.

HER GENEROSITY and CHARITABLE BUILDING WORKS

Miss Thomas was very keen on education and built a number of Pencerrig schools, including the one at Beulah, in 1849 and apparently she gave much time and attention to the pupils. It was called the Llwyn Madoc C P School; this rather surprised my four children who all started their education there at the age of four or five!

Another example of her benefaction was her involvement in the building of the Hospital in Llandrindod Wells. She joined the original committee of gentry and clergy in 1877. The Thomas family became generous annual subscribers and, together with the Venables family of Llysdinam, who were kinsmen, provided a third of the funds collected by 1880. She served on the first Ladies' Committee, and she bore the entire cost of the convalescent wing which was added in 1883, and endowed it with £3,000 for increased expenses. It is thought that this might have been as a memorial to the brother who had died so tragically 20 years before. This seems likely because high on the west gable is the Thomas coat of arms, and under them the initials E.L.T. which were Evan's initials.

In 1908 she served as President of the Hospital and she gave a further addition, a detached Mortuary. She also donated £1,000 to the building of Builth Wells Cottage Hospital, which was not built until 1897.

I wonder what she would think now that is has been demolished, and is sadly missed throughout the area.

She was also passionate about building churches. Among others, she built the large church at Abergwesyn (where many of the Thomas family are buried) and where the Llwyn Madoc family worshipped until she built Eglwys Oen Duw in 1866, which lies exactly half way between Llwyn Madoc and the village of Beulah. Why? Because she didn't want the people from the village to travel any further than she had to. How typical of her thoughtfulness.

Unfortunately, her taste was often inspired by the churches and buildings that she so loved in Italy where she spent time travelling and studying the art of the Treasures of Florence, Rome and Venice. Some of the materials used did not stand up to the rigorous winters in the hills of mid Wales, and the church at Abergwesyn was pulled down in the nineteen fifties because the stone was porous.

She made many improvements to both her houses; notably the addition of the servants' quarters at Pencerrig. When some alterations to the main reception rooms were in progress recently, a small card was found behind the wainscotting; on it was written, 'This oak dado was in Builth Church for about 200 years, and was altered and fixed here by Shoolbred and Co., London, September 1882'. This panelling must then have been done to the orders of Miss Thomas. St. Mary's Church in Builth Wells had been largely rebuilt in 1875-1876 at a cost of some £5,000, to which Miss Thomas, as patroness, contributed £1,000, as well as adding a stained glass east window to the memory of her mother, who died in 1877, but it was not dedicated until 1887.

It would seem that the oak panelling had been removed from the old church, and not being used in the new church, had later been sold to Miss Thomas for use at Pencerrig.

HER CHARACTER AND GENEROSITY

That she had another side to her nature is revealed by a story, possibly apocryphal. Advised that the lake at Pencerrig needed cleaning out, she is supposed to have hired a gang of Irish navvies to do the job, just at the time that David Lloyd George's Unemployment Insurance Bill was passed. She so disapproved of the 'advanced ideas of the Welsh politician' that she sent the navvies packing, and the cleaning of the lake was never done!

I well remember a lovely old lady, Winnie Blythe, who lived in Beulah, telling me how Miss Thomas' carriage stopped outside her house one day. Winnie was only about fifteen and she always said that Miss Thomas prodded her gently and told her that she should come to work in the Llwyn Madoc kitchens, which she did for many years. She told me this as though the Queen had visited her house.

Of course nowadays this would be treated as grossly impertinent but then, in days of unemployment and hardship it was accepted as a kindness and a privilege. Just think, if I had done that, half a century later, it would have been headlines in the local paper!

For those not old enough to recall a way of life that has now gone for ever, there is a vivid, though perhaps biased description, of Pencerrig and Llwyn Madoc under the regime of Miss Thomas in Vaughan's Squires of South Wales (1926), at a time when she owned over 14,000 acres of land in Breconshire, Radnorshire and Glamorgan, with a gross annual rental of £5,000.

I have also heard her described as not only rich, but devout and immensely formidable; almost as a legend in her own time;

a model landlord, and that she lived a life of inner virtue and selflessness. The list is endless, and we have seen time and again how her daily life was conducted on old-fashioned principles.

HOSPITALITY

It must be said that although her many duties took up much time and attention, this amazing lady also enjoyed an outward life of hospitality. During the summer months an endless procession of visitors filled Llwyn Madoc to enjoy croquet, tennis, fishing, shooting, walking, picnics, billiards and card-playing. It was a self-contained community with twenty four souls sleeping beneath the roof. Between all the fun and entertainment, there were always morning and evening prayers, and music and singing, often with the servants in attendance.

As we read at the beginning in 'The Little Trolley', Miss Thomas and her entourage spent the summers at Llwyn Madoc, and then moved in a mighty cavalcade down the valley to Pencerrig. Harriet James who as a child had lived with her parents at the Home Farm said that what impressed her most was the annual Fancy Dress Ball held in the New Year, at which there would be some hundred guests and a large orchestra. The house would be hung with many lanterns, and the following night was the Staff Ball, with hours of delight whirling round to the strains of the waltzes, so beloved by the Victorians.

So although she was extremely well off, Miss Thomas was not only immensely generous to the many causes which she championed, but also spent her time, as well as money, to support and encourage them. The life she lived was dutiful, useful, unselfish and spontaneous. Never a day seemed to pass without some act of kindness or help or support for someone in need. Nothing seemed to be too much trouble for her, and yet in spite of all her wealth, her own needs were minimal, and she could well be described as stringent almost frugal.

HER SPIRITUALITY

The great interest Miss Thomas took in 'religious' and educational matters is on record. However, unlike some of her ancestors who had staunch Nonconformist tendencies during the 18th and 19th centuries, Miss Thomas and her close family were devout Anglicans. Almost certainly she showed as much hospitality to the clergy of the established church as her forebears had done to their Nonconformist ministers.

> She remained throughout her long life a staunch supporter of the established Church of England, as it still was, and like those before her, she certainly followed in the family's tradition and gave unstintingly not only her money, but also her time.
>
> I sometimes wonder whether, had she lived a century earlier, she might have embraced her forebears' Nonconformist views. Who knows? Whatever course she took, she would most certainly have served her Maker with her whole heart and soul, mind and spirit.

HER APPEARANCE

Whatever can be said of this fine lady, surely no-one can doubt the incredible duty of her nature and the generosity of her spirit.

Not only did she possess a fine character, but she was also known to be of beautiful appearance and she was certainly attractive: Kilvert refers to her in his diary for February 1870, at a dinner party at Clyro Court, when she was twenty eight, as '*Looking very pretty and nice in a blue silk dress; she sat opposite me at dinner and afterwards when we came into the drawing room, she came up and shook hands cordially and kindly talked 'till the Baskerville's carriage was announced. It was a very happy evening.*'

Photograph of Clara Thomas in later life

HER SUITORS

There was no shortage of suitors, but one man in particular had wanted to marry her for many years: he was Henry William Harper, born in 1833 at Eton, where he went to school before going on to graduate at Oxford. His family, if not distantly related to the Thomases, were at least very long-standing friends. He was ordained in 1856 and served the next seven years in the Church of New Zealand. It is said that she never married for fear that she might transmit the disease which killed her mother, but I had always heard that Miss Thomas never married him because it meant going to live in New Zealand. This she clearly would not do as she felt it her duty to manage her estates in Wales.

The Archdeacon came back to England in 1864 and acted as Commissary to his father, Bishop Harper, for 3 years, during which time he paid his unsuccessful court to Miss Thomas. He returned

Clara Thomas' grave and wheel cross at Eglwys Oen Duw (The Church of the Lamb of God), Beulah.

to New Zealand and ministered there until his retirement in 1911 as Archdeacon. He came back again to England and, though he made London his home, he spent a great deal of time at Llwyn Madoc, and he was one of the distinguished mourners at the funeral of Miss Thomas in June 1914, in the churchyard of Eglwys Oen Duw. He may well have been at her bedside during her last days in a London nursing home, where she died after a serious operation. He himself died in Kensington in 1922.

I find it incredibly poignant that Archdeacon Harper made it quite clear in his will that he would like to be buried at the foot of the grave of Clara Thomas. This wish was granted, and it gives me a warm feeling every time I see his grave in our churchyard, at the foot of the grave as requested, close to all the other Evan-Thomas and Bourdillon family graves at Eglwys Oen Duw. He surely must have been totally devoted to her.

Archdeacon Harper's grave
(at the foot of Clara Thomas' grave as requested in his will.)

Clara Thomas' signature in 1901

Chapter 7

AFTER MISS THOMAS' DEATH

PENCERRIG

At Miss Thomas' death in 1914, Pencerrig passed to the eldest son of Mrs. N. Lindsay, whose paternal grandfather, the Rev. George Thomas of Ystrad Fawr in Llanfabon, Glamorgan, was the younger brother of Thomas Thomas of Llanbradach and Pencerrig. Mrs. Lindsay was the wife of Col. H. E. Morgan Lindsay, a grandson of the first Lord Tredegar. The Lindsays only used Pencerrig for brief summer holidays, but for a time they entertained lavishly, especially in the fishing and shooting seasons, their guests including many ambassadors, and among other notabilities, Sir Robert Baden-Powell.

Pencerrig was thus becoming very run down when in September 1928, and on hearing that the whole Lindsay estate in Radnorshire was to be sold, Mr. Llewelyn Evan-Thomas, (the third son of Charles Evan-Thomas, who had died at his home at The Gnoll, Neath), purchased that part of the estate lying east of the Dulas brook. This included Pencerrig and its Diserth and Llanelwedd farms, but excluded the Caerwnon area west of the Dulas, for which Mr. Ralph Woosnam acted as agent. Mr. Evan-Thomas, who married a Miss Booker of Velindre, Glamorgan, had spent most of his adult life in Antwerp in charge of a large shipping business, and he now retired to a country house only some ten miles from Llwyn Madoc: the home of his ancestors (Pencerrig). As early as 1918 the Llewelyn Evan-Thomases had rented from Sir Charles Venables-Llewelyn his Newbridge-on-Wye property of Brynwern, so they were well acquainted with the area, and they were now spending far more time there than in Antwerp.

After rescuing Pencerrig in 1929 when it was in a bad state of repair, Mr. and Mrs. Llewelyn Evan-Thomas took up residence and renovated the house, the original drive and its lodge. Meanwhile their son, Charles Lindsay Evan-Thomas, who had, like his first cousin also called Charles, followed a career in the Royal Navy, resigned his commission, with the rank of Commander, to take his father's place in Antwerp.

However the outbreak of World War II, in 1939, meant his recall to the Navy, and he served with distinction on the Dover Patrol. During the war his mother died, but his father stayed on at Pencerrig, where Charles brought his bride, the former Miss Jane Kemp of Sussex, in 1947.

In the same year, Llewelyn Evan-Thomas, died at the age of 87, and his son Charles, who had taken an active part in many sides of local life, died only 3 years later. All were buried in Cwmbach Llechryd church, which had been built by Clara Thomas, about a mile, equidistant, from Pencerrig and Caerwnon (another Thomas house built a little further up on the banks of the river Wye). The folk from Pencerrig considered it their 'Home Church' and they worshipped there every Sunday when in residence. It must have been quite a sight seeing the entire family arriving each Sunday.

Charles' widow Jane Evan-Thomas lived on at Pencerrig until 1952 when it was left to Timothy Stileman who never lived there, and he sold it to Messrs. David and Robert Tudor of Trawsfynydd, Merionethshire as a business venture. They felled the mature timber, but rarely if ever used Pencerrig as a home, so once again the house began to deteriorate.

Pencerrig still contained numerous reminders of Thomas Jones the Artist, including many of his paintings and sketch books. The drawings in some of the sketch books are of scenes around the house, even small details of which can be readily recognised today, some 180 years after they were first drawn.

Pages from the sketchbook of Thomas Jones

When Pencerrig came on the market again in 1958 most of the farms on the estate were sold to the sitting tenants whose families in many cases had held them for several generations.

Pencerrig house itself was finally sold to Mr. Carrel of Builth, whose wife was a native of the locality, and they converted it into a Country Hotel, specialising in pony trekking.

So in 1969 Pencerrig was lively again with the sound of young voices, like those of the brood of Thomas and Hannah Jones 200 years before; but instead of hunters, the stables then housed sturdy Welsh cobs, and after a day out trekking over Carneddau, a string of tired but happy and hungry visitors could be seen any summer evening wending its way homewards across the one-time deer park up to 'The House at the top of the Rocks'.

The Brecon and Radnorshire Branch of the WHGT was alerted to Pencerrig's recent demise, where high wire mesh gates were erected by the main Lodge. A site visit found that the house and gardens had gone to rack and ruin.

The owner objected aggressively to any enquiries made so it is very worrying that the fine old 18th house as well as the landscape so well documented by Thomas Jones is now at risk of becoming a lost landscape.

LWYN MADOC

Meantime what became of her other 'House up the Valley' after Miss Thomas' death?

The Llwyn Madoc estate went to her second cousin, (Henry) Algernon, whose grandfather, Charles, was younger brother of Henry Thomas of Llwyn Madoc (who had by deed poll in 1881 assumed the surname of Evan-Thomas). Charles was the father of another Algernon, married to Lilian Lee, who lived at Caerwnon and they produced six children, of whom the first four were girls, followed by two boys, (Henry) Algernon and

Charles (Marmaduke). The eldest girl Gwyneth married Lance Lewin, and the second, Lilian, married a Mr. Stileman, then Cara (my mother-in-law) was number three, married to the Revd. Gerard Bourdillon, and the fourth sister Kathleen married Ralph Woosnam of Cefnllysgwynne, another notable house in the area, once owned by Miss Thomas, and is still enjoyed by the Woosnam family. (Their son Charles, born in 1925, ran with Norman Tyler the highly regarded Land Agents Woosnam and Tyler in Builth Wells for many years, and it still happily continues as Chester Master.)

The first brother, (Henry) Algernon, known as Algy, succeeded Miss Thomas at Llwyn Madoc when she died, in 1914. He had married Nancy Roundell of Garth House. The Wilson family arrived at Garth House in 1910, since when there has been a close friendship with the folk at Llwyn Madoc, and which Mervyn and I enjoyed for over sixty years. It is a great delight to me that this has carried on to the present generation, which continues with Mathew and Caroline Wilson to this day. Think back for a moment to Marmaduke Gwynne if you don't remember the link between these two houses in the 18th century.

Algy (as he was always known) was wounded in World War II but only died in 1939 , with no issue, so Llwyn Madoc passed to his younger brother Charles (Marmaduke) who inherited Llwyn Madoc in 1939, but went straight off to fight in the Royal Navy in World War II, during which time the house was used as a school for children with physical difficulties.

Incidentally much of the furniture from the house, including family papers, were stored above the stables where there was a horrific fire in 1939 so no doubt a lot of the history was lost. I remember a dear man, Mendel Meredith, who ran the excellent Watts Clothiers in Builth telling me how, as a fireman, he had spent the whole night up a ladder, trying to save the building, but it was impossible. [This was a particular tragedy for me personally that the beautiful stables had gone, because we had endless horses and ponies, which were my passion, all the time I lived at Llwyn Madoc. However we later renovated the old cow house into four nice loose boxes, which made all the difference to my life.]

Commander Charles (as he then was) returned to Llwyn Madoc after the war with his Canadian wife Evva, but he died very suddenly and unexpectedly in 1953, also with no issue, and there were no more males of that generation. So what next?

It was left in male entail to his nephew, Mervyn Bourdillon, who died in 2002; hence the name Bourdillon suddenly appears, but his mother was an Evan-Thomas so it is still a direct line from the original family of Thomases. Mervyn wrote this;

Mervyn Bourdillon

'There were no male heirs of that generation and I was somewhat surprised to receive a telegram in 1953, while I was working in a family firm in the Sudan, telling me to come back and run Llwyn Madoc. Although I thought I would be called upon to do so at some stage of my life, none of us expected my uncle to die very suddenly at the age of 56, so it all happened much earlier than anticipated.'

So we are now back to the beginning when I mentioned that Mervyn and I married in 1961 and how we had had the immense pleasure and privilege of living in such a beautiful family house for over forty years. We left Llwyn Madoc in 2001 and handed over to the next generation.

Mervyn was Lord-Lieutenant of Powys from 1985 to 1999, and died in 2002.

Our son Patrick and his wife Miranda took over in 2001 and still live there with their three lovely daughters. I rather think that he, Patrick, might be heartened to learn something that I read recently how the 'upkeep of a house was as worrying then (1792) as it is now'! Mervyn certainly found it a constant anxiety, and it is probably even worse now, but at least it is a happy home and a well-maintained house, and let us hope and trust that it will never fall into the shameful disrepair that has ravaged Pencerrig in these latter years.

****

I suppose our story ends there, but while doing the research on Pencerrig I have become more and more interested by the events leading up to the local Welsh Revival of 1769, and the characters involved in bringing it about. I had no idea that Howell Harris ever visited Pencerrig, let alone many times; or that so much of the Pencerrig story is intrinsically linked with this incredible Movement. I have found it fascinating.

People speak often of the astonishing happenings during the great Welsh Revival in 1904, but so much of this local eighteenth century Revival seems to have been rather lost in the mists of time, other than by students of that period.

There are a few overlaps (duplication) which I have not omitted, because unless you were particularly attentive reading about people like Howell Harris and Marmaduke Gwynne in Chapter 5, I felt it would bear a little repetition in certain places.

Caebach Chapel Stable by Marcia Gibson-Watt

PART TWO

DISSENT AND THE NONCONFORMISTS

DISSENT AND THE NONCONFORMISTS

Taken from a talk given by Tanya Jenkins
in Caebach Chapel on 11th June, 2022

Since writing about these astonishing men I had the good fortune to meet Tanya Jenkins who explained to me very succinctly the difference between what we now call 'Nonconformist' denominations. At last I understand the difference between what we now call Nonconformism and Dissention.

The early Dissenters actually rebelled against the established church, as they were motivated by their desire to return to a purer form of Christian faith and church structure, based firmly on their interpretation of the Bible. The two movements, which were the most significant in Wales at this time, were the Baptists and the Independents, also known as Congregationalists. Their number increased during the Civil War period. However they were greatly persecuted during the early years of the Restoration following the passing of the 4 Acts of the Clarendon Code, which were designed to cripple their power and influence. As a result, many emigrated to America, where they had more freedom.

The Act of Toleration in 1689 made things easier for the Dissenters in this country, and they were then allowed to meet in small numbers: hence the emergence of House groups.

It is thought that David Jones, when he returned from London to Wales following the Civil War, was a Dissenter and worshipped with the group that met at Y Garn farm, although he was also Warden of Cefnllys Parish Church, and is buried there. Of his two sons, John, the eldest who inherited his estate, followed his father in becoming Warden at Cefnllys and is also interred there. However, the younger son Thomas was a

Dissenter who attended the Dissenting Academy at Shrewsbury, as his beliefs would have precluded him from attending Oxford or Cambridge. Upon completing his education there he became a Dissenting Minister at Tetbury in Gloucestershire, where he built the Independent Meeting House there at his own expense. Returning home to Trefonnen on a regular basis, he also built the Independent Caebach chapel, which still stands on the perimeter of Llandrindod Wells

In 1735 there was a sea change in religion in Wales due to what came to be known as The Methodist Revival. John Wesley was very methodical, hence the name Methodist; he and his brother Charles were Arminians, and not Calvinists like George Whitefield.

Initially, the Methodists were all members of the Church of England; they were not Dissenters and had no wish to establish a separate Church. The Methodist Revival began in Wales with the spiritual awakening of Howell Harris of Trefecca, and the Revd. Daniel Rowland of Llangeitho. The famous Welsh hymn writer, author of the hymn 'Bread of Heaven;' the Revd. William Williams, Pantycelyn, was spiritually awakened by hearing Howell Harris speaking or 'exhorting' as it was known, in the burial ground of the church in Trefecca. Together, these three men became known as the Methodist leaders in Wales.

REVIVAL

The year is 1769. The ladies among you sitting here would be wearing bonnets and long skirts and the gentlemen, jackets, breeches, cravats, wigs or hats. But you wouldn't be sitting quite so sedately as you are today. In fact, some of you would not be sitting at all – but jumping up and down, whilst others would be kneeling and weeping. Others would be proclaiming in loud voices your gratitude for being washed in God's saving grace.

Why? In that year, this little congregational chapel, Caebach, was gripped by a new wave of the Methodist Revival, and up there in the pulpit was the Minister proclaiming the mercy of God and the necessity of being saved from damnation for all he was worth.

"The Spirit of the Lord came down in an extraordinary way about the year 1769, just as on the day of Pentecost. It caused many to cry out under conviction, while others blessed the Lord with singing and praying, and each one speaking with his neighbour. The people of the world were amazed."

Things continued like this during the years 1770 to 1772, so that news of the success of Caebach Chapel, Llandrindod Wells spread throughout all Wales.

"So that's my theme for today, says Tanya; how this little congregational chapel in the eighteenth century, thanks to its founding family, became such a hotbed/volcano of Methodist activity, spreading its hot lava of religious revival to surrounding Radnorshire and beyond. Reminders of the founding family of Trefonnen have pride of place for us here today...

"David Jones of Erwddalen, Llanfihangel Bryn Pabuan in Breconshire returned from London and bought Trefonnen, here in the parish of Cefnllys. David had two sons, John and Thomas. John, as the eldest, was the heir to the estate and devoted his effort to its cultivation and growth, becoming High Sheriff of Radnorshire in 1737."

EDUCATION

The youngest son in such circumstances would be set for a career in religion, and so Thomas was sent to study at the Dissenting Academy at Shrewsbury. From 1662 until the mid-nineteenth century it was not possible to take a degree at either Oxford or Cambridge without taking the Oath of Supremacy and or subscribing to the Thirty-Nine Articles of the Church of England, which Dissenting families preferred not to do.

The Dissenting academies offered a very high standard of education, with a curriculum which offered not only biblical studies but also Greek, Hebrew, Latin, mathematics, philosophy, geography and literature. Shrewsbury Academy was established by the Revd. James Owen, originally in Oswestry in 1690 and moved to Shrewsbury in 1700. This James Owen, the principal tutor, was acknowledged as one of the most outstanding scholars of his time; it is said that he lectured to his students in Latin, and indeed he expected them to chat with one another in Latin whilst eating their dinner!

THOMAS and ELIZABETH JONES

Following his education, Thomas accepted a call to a congregationalist chapel in Tetbury in Gloucestershire, the foundation of which followed a local ejected Anglican minister licensing his own home in Tetbury for preaching in 1672.

According to local sources in Tetbury, the Revd. Thomas Jones built the meeting house there at his own expense in the early 1700s. In 1713, he married Elizabeth Middleton Hope from Llandrindod Hall, Trefonnen's neighbouring estate: another family with strong Dissenting connections. Elizabeth's family owned Y Garn in neighbouring Disserth, the location of one of the earliest Dissenting gatherings in the community. The congregation was said to have numbered around 200 in 1715 – with 30 of them voters – in other words, landowners. This included the Jones family themselves.

CAEBACH CHAPEL

The Revd. Thomas Jones of Tetbury returned frequently to Trefonnen – and it was around this time it is said that he funded the building of Caebach, both for his own convenience and also as an alternative meeting place for those who worshipped at the farmhouse Y Garn. Exact dates of the establishment vary, but the majority seem to suggest that Caebach was built around the same time, 1715. The Revd. Christodocius Lewis, educated at Carmarthen Dissenting Academy, was the first minister to be appointed there.

As we have already learned, Thomas and Elizabeth, good strong Dissenters, had one surviving daughter, Hannah, born in 1721, and in 1738, when she was just 17, she was married to her first cousin, John's son, also called Thomas, at St Mary's Church in Gloucester. Strong in their dissenting beliefs just like their forebears, Thomas and Hannah's peaceful lives (aged 27 and 17) at Trefonnen, and the life of this quiet chapel were about to change radically, with the advent of the Methodist Revival.

Enter Howell Harris from Trefecca.

HOWELL HARRIS

There is no doubt that Howell Harris' spiritual awakening after receiving communion at his parish in Talgarth in 1735, **changed Wales.** It may seem almost inconceivable that the spiritual experience of one individual can have such an extensive impact on the history and character of a nation, but it did, through the spread of his 'Methodist Way':

> *Religion was no longer a doctrinal or liturgical exercise,*
> *but a real personal relationship with the Saviour, Jesus Christ.*

He did not set out to create a separate denomination, but rather to revive the spiritual life of the vast majority of people who attended their local parish church. Despite many efforts to seek ordination he was always refused, so Harris was not allowed to preach inside the church as he was not ordained, and so initially he began preaching – or exhorting or discoursing as it was called – in churchyards and private homes. As the extent of people who were spiritually awakened continued to grow, they were formed into small local groups called Societies, and local leaders were appointed from among them to oversee their spiritual progress and report back to meetings of the leaders, called Associations.

Harris himself was, quite literally, a man on a mission. Anyone who has read his diaries, or even just his itinerary, cannot fail to be astonished at the ground he literally covered, as he travelled the length and breadth of the country, calling people to a spiritual awakening.

It is must be said that neither he, nor any of the other exhorters and proponents of the new Methodist Way, were popular in public, and they often faced strong local opposition from rabble rousers gathered for the express purpose of disrupting their speaking. This shows how courageous they were in face of what was sometimes dangerous opposition.

MARMADUKE GWYNNE

A technique used to silence the Methodists was to have them arrested by getting the local Magistrate to read the Riot Act. The most famous example is that of the aristocratic Marmaduke Gwynne, the squire of Garth who was born nearby in Llanafan fawr in 1691 We have already heard of him, in chapter 5.

Hearing that Harris was about to preach in his locality, he famously went to listen, in the role of an investigating magistrate. He took with him a copy of the Riot Act, the reading of which was a necessary preliminary to dispersing an assembly thought to be contrary to public order. However, with the need to presume innocence, he first had to listen to one of Harris' sermons.

To his immense surprise, Gwynne was an immediate convert, and even invited Harris back to his mansion to eat that evening, to the disgust of his family; his wife refused to eat with the stranger. But his eleven year old daughter Sally was intrigued.

| (Do you see the significance of this? Read on!)

In 1738 Gwynne was offering the use of valuable books in Welsh, and he was considered to be amongst the first members of the gentry in Wales openly to declare their support for this religious revolution. Meanwhile only his daughter shared his spiritual confidence in this household.

JOHN JONES and the FAMILY of TREFONNEN

The Jones family of Trefonnen, as already established, were a minor gentry family with strong Dissenting connections. Sadly it is not known how or when the Trefonnen family first came into contact with Harris himself, but from the itinerary composed from the entries in Harris' diary, it seemed that by 1740, he had increased his circular exhorting routes to take in the Radnorshire area, travelling to Rhaeadr and Llandrindod. Harris was very particular about recording where he visited, and on July 19th 1740, he records for the first time that he stayed at Trefonnen in Radnorshire, the Jones family home As it is a Sunday, it is more than possible that he preached here in this chapel for the first time. It seems that the Jones family thoroughly embraced this new spiritual way – and Harris himself as the following example shows.

In the Quarter Session held in Presteigne on 8 October 1740, Harris was due to appear on a charge of 'riotous assault'. Prior to the case, with the threat of imprisonment playing on his mind, he noted: *'Last night in no bed at all but slept about three hours by the fire. At 7 went toward Presteigne, about 8 or 10 miles. About 9 saw Mr. Jones of Trefonnen's son, (none other than our friend Marmaduke Gwynne) – a Justice's son – whose heart the Lord inclined to come to Sessions to take care of me and be my friend'.*

A little later, he writes: *'Stirring up Mr. Gwynne's heart to be concerned for me to write to a Counsellor and promising to come and assist me with person and purse… Stirring up Mr Jones of Trefonnen… to send to Sir Humphrey Howarth (the local MP) to say that he would assist me in expenses and to send his son to take care of me. Stirring up 4 to Bail me that are Brethren willing fully to spend and be spent and one of them to go to Sir H Howarth and Mr. Jones' son for an attorney.'*

Here is an example of the Jones family of Trefonnen actually being there to support Harris in his court appearance, being willing to plead his case if necessary with the local MP and to fund his bail.

The case against Harris failed to secure an acquittal, and the case was transferred to the next Quarter Sessions, to be held at Knighton on the 14-15th January 1741. After staying overnight at Llandegley an understandably exhausted Harris left for Trefonnen, presumably with the young Mr Jones, to recuperate and recorded in his notes: *'Came to Trefonnen. Conversing with the dear soul Mrs. Jones, when she talked of their building a Meeting House. I found bigotry in me. Later prayed for the Meeting House. Slept about 3 hours.'* When the case was heard at Knighton the following January, Harris is advised by both Marmaduke Gwynne and his lawyer to plead guilty and ask for pardon; however the verdict was delayed as the court members apparently all went to the pub – presumably to drink the good health of the accused! Eventually Harris is fined 11/6 and set free to go. He commented *"I was made a spectacle here. Praise the Lord for this honour."*

When Harris left the court he was seized by a riotous mob intent on murder. Gwynne and his brother, Roderick Gwynne of Glanbran, were able to avoid a lynching. Marmaduke had been able to use his skill and influence to avoid a custodial sentence, but Harris had to pay a fine for a reduced charge of *'behaving in a riotous manner.'*

It seems that the Gwynnes and the Jones', two very influential local families, worked together to shelter and support Harris, especially in the early days of his ministry.

This was just the beginning of Howell Harris' lifetime connection with the Jones family, and over the following years he visits Trefonnen fourteen times. As his exhorting circuits took him further and further afield the visits became less, however there is no doubt whatsoever that in those early days, Howell Harris himself preached in Caebach chapel, and from all accounts, with no small degree of success.

On Sunday 29th October 1769, (remember the date!) he commented:

'To Caebach meeting House past ten. Found a large congregation gathered and singing in the meeting house and in the church yard and strong gales of life… I met many that had been awakened through me in these parts 30 years ago.'

John Jones senior, or the Justice, as he was called by Howell Harris died in 1746 and Trefonnen passed to his son, Thomas and his wife Hannah. During this time however, the popularity of Llandrindod as a holiday destination has grown exponentially due to the popularity of the waters, and Thomas and Hannah and their young family left for the estate of Pencerrig near Builth, which was part of Hannah's inheritance. Despite leaving Llandrindod however, it is noted that they, along with their numerous children, sixteen altogether, (although a number did not survive childhood) all worshipped at Caebach on a Sunday.

MINISTERS at CAEBACH CHAPEL

The Revd. Christodocius Lewis left Caebach in 1752 and was followed by John Evans, said to have been one of the Caebach's own flock. In 1755, the congregation formed a joint pastorate with the *Independent* cause at Rhaeadr, under the ministry of the Revd. Simon Williams of Tredwstan.

Rev. JOHN (IOAN) THOMAS

In 1767 probably Caebach's most noted minister was appointed, fresh from the congregational dissenting academy in Abergavenny, his education having been funded by the Congregational Fund. However, in reality denominationalism and ecclesiology meant very little to this remarkable individual, who considered himself to be the spiritual son of Howell Harris and who was an absolutely fervent adherent to the Methodist Way.

Revd. John Thomas was minister, travelling preacher, author of a number of surprisingly well-known Welsh language hymns, which are still sung today, and above all, the author of the very first Welsh language autobiography, **Rhad Ras.** Which means **Free Grace**.

Known locally as Ioan, due to his small stature, he was born in a small cottage called 'Col' on the border of Llanddeusant and Myddfai, in 1730. The parish register of Myddfai records that he was baptised on April 25th of that year, and that his parents were not married, which sadly made him a social outcast. He was raised by a loving aunt, however she died when he was eight and he was moved around various relatives for food and lodging.

A melancholy child, he felt his rejection from his immediate family very keenly and referred to himself in his autobiography as

> *'y gwaelaf a mwyaf distadl o dŷ fy nhad:*
> *the lowest and most insignificant of my father's house'.*

He also had severe epilepsy; one of his convulsions as a child almost killed him and left him critically ill for a month or more. One can only begin to imagine the superstitious attitudes and beliefs of an uneducated community as it sought to find reasons for these strange fits. His epilepsy continued in adulthood, and he himself recounted that he found himself waking up in a hedgerow, without any idea whatsoever how he had got there.

When he was thirteen years old in 1743, he began work as a *gwas bach* at Gellifelen Farm. Whilst there he got first wind of something unusual: he heard the son of the house praying extempory prayers without using the prayer book. Gellifelen Farm was on the road between two places of well-known Methodist gatherings, the home of Jeffrey Dafydd Ifan at Rhiwie, Llanddeusant and the Methodist meeting at Cefn Telyrch in Myddfai.

Howell Harris, who himself was known to have been a regular visitor at both places (he visited 12 times between the years of 1738 and 1743) and so the young John Thomas went to hear him preach at the home of Jeffrey Dafydd Ifan, Rhiwie, Llanddeusant in February 1743. The sermon had such an impact on him, he could remember it and quoted it 60 years later.

> *"Oni chaiff Duw dy galon di fe fyn weled*
> *y diawliaid yn dy rwygo gorff ac enaid*
> *yn awr angau ac yn nydd y farn."*

*"If God does not have your heart, he will want to see
the devils ripping you apart, body and soul
at the hour of death and in the day of judgement."*

A few days later, after meditating on the sermon, John experienced a striking conversion experience, which was to change the course of his life. He wrote:

'Mi ges y trysor gorau A feddai'r nef ei hun,
sef undeb priodasol â Iesu Mab y Dyn.'

'I received heaven's greatest treasure,
a matrimonial union with Jesus the Son of God.'

From then on, John considered Howell Harris to be his father in the faith. In his Marwnad elegy that he wrote for him, he described him thus:

'Pan yn blentyn ces ei wrando,
Rhyw olwg rhyfedd cefais arno,
Mi dybiais fod ei wedd yn rhyw-fodd
Fel wyneb angel fry o'r nefoedd;
Pan ddechreuodd â tharanu
Llawer oedd o'i flaen yn crynu
Minnau'r gwan, yn y man
'Deimlodd ran o'i saethau,
Nes own yn profi dymuniadau
Am ei ganlyn ffordd y cerddai.'

'When I was a child, I got to listen to him;
I saw that he was of a wondrous appearance,
like an angel from heaven.
When he began to thunder,
many people before him began to shake;
and myself, as a weak person there,
and then began to feel his arrows;
until I too wished to walk in his way.'

However, consoled as he was, the whole experience didn't help John Thomas to make friends and keep them; rather it engendered in him a strong but rather unfortunate feeling of self-righteousness, and with all the enthusiasm of a convert, a burning desire to point out to others the error of their ways. This tendency never left him, as we shall soon discover.

It first manifested in his dissatisfaction with the behaviour of people in Myddfai parish. In common with many other parishes in Wales, whilst waiting for the Vicar or Curate to come and lead the Sunday Service, the people of Myddfai amused themselves by playing games in the churchyard – in this case, quoits. The thirteen year old John complained bitterly to the churchwardens about this but they apparently could not be bothered to come out of the pub and do anything about it. In the end, he found out where the quoits were kept and confiscated them himself. As a biographer recounts that this was done 'with evident satisfaction but at some possible danger to himself had the players found out that he was responsible'.

In 1745, fifteen year old John was delighted to have secured a new appointment as a servant to Griffith Jones, Llanddowror: *"His speech and appearance won my heart and it was as though I had seen an angel of God."*

He wanted to follow in Howell Harris' footsteps and possibly even wanted to try for Anglican orders, but Griffith Jones diplomatically suggested that maybe he would be better off as a teacher. The result was that young John was sent to study for a year with none other than Howell Harris at Trefecca, and following this, he was employed in various schools. During this time he began to preach, and had some success in effecting spiritual awakenings in others: his first converts being members of his own family. Unsuccessful in his attempts to take holy orders in the Anglican Church, and with the assistance of a congregational minister called the Revd. Joseph Simmons, he applied for ministry in the Congregational church, and was funded by the Congregational Fund to attend their academy in Abergavenny between 1761 and 1766. He often complained of the lukewarmness of his fellow students, and was always glad to escape to Llangeitho during the holidays; once again to be among people of the same fervent spiritual ilk, especially following what came to be known as the Sea of Glass or Llangeitho Revival from 1762 to 1764.

After leaving Abergavenny, John Thomas was first called to Brychgoed Chapel near Heol Senni; it was established by the Revd. Edmund Jones of Pontypool, another Congregationalist minister with very strong Methodist leanings. However, after six months there, he was rejected as being too much of a Methodist. He was then called to minister at Caebach, and at Rhaeadr, and Y Garn – no small coincidence when one considers the connection between himself and the Jones family and Howell Harris. He was ordained on 23rd April 1767, in a service which featured the three most ardent 'Methodist' congregationalist ministers of the day: the Reverends Edmund Jones, Isaac Price and Richard Tibbot.

John Thomas had little in the way of worldly possessions, but Hannah Jones, formerly of Trefonnen, now of Pencerrig, had a strong admiration for him, which seemed to have been mutual, and she personally sponsored him. He notes that he often visited the family at Pencerrig and in a touching and very revealing note, he commented that Hannah and her husband Thomas *"were like a mother and father to my wife and me."*

It seemed that her beliefs concurred very much with those of John Thomas himself. He said of her, *"Many times I heard her with pleasure, speaking of Christ and his complete Salvation, for an hour together, more like a divine than a private Christian".* Her beliefs translated into a spirit of worldly generosity because at Pencerrig, according to John Thomas, she kept *"an open house and an open heart to receive the poor, to feed the hungry and clothe the naked."*

This generosity extended to John Thomas himself, as he was paid a salary of around £10 a year for his ministry by Madam Jones, in addition to various homes in the area, including Llannerchdirion, now the Llannerch Inn behind Tesco. His salary was in keeping with the local Anglican stipend; in 1791 the diary of Thomas Jones the Artist notes on June 18[th,] *'Paid curate of Llandrindod one year's salary due 31st May – £10.'*

The following year, 1768, Howell Harris came to visit John Thomas at Caebach and then in 1769, two years into John Thomas' ministry, a celebrated revival broke out in the chapel. The account is outlined in Rhad Ras:

'The Spirit of the Lord came down in an extraordinary way during the ministry of the Word in about the year 1769, just as on the day of Pentecost, in our public and private meetings, especially during the sharing of the Lord's Supper. It caused many to cry out under conviction, while others blessed the Lord with singing and praying, and each one speaking with his neighbour. The people of the world were amazed, and were several times unable to leave during the Sabbath until I returned having preached in Rhayader, travelling about twenty miles there and back again. The stirring spread throughout the neighbourhood, and added to the church I separated four in the Caebach church to be deacons and elders, and three of the young men also, with the consent of the church, to use their gifts publicly, as assistants in the flourishing church and so things continued like this during the years 1770, 1771, and 1772, so that news of the success of Caebach near the wells (ie: Llandrindod Wells) spread throughout all Wales.'

It was a wonderful time in Caebach:
the fields were white unto harvest.

However, as is often the case in life, not everyone was happy with the revivalist situation at Caebach. From his black and white perspective, John Thomas viewed those who opposed him as instruments of the devil – and feeling in need of some support, he did what he had done before – he turned to his father in the faith, Howell Harris. On 9 June 1769, John Thomas wrote to Howell Harris:

'Honoured and Dear Sir,

The devil is disturbed in our parts and is a-roaring in the prophane and professors more than I have seen him since I came here. Sometimes in Rhaeadr we have the stones thrown towards the windows of the Meeting House – but in Caebach, the prince of darkness is awakened in great fury in our parts – and my desire is that the Lord of the Harvest would send you here and come with you to put him down…Dear Mr Harris don't forget us but come and give us your assisting hand both at Rhaeadr and Caebach as soon as possible and may the Prince of Light come with you.'

Happily, Howell Harris responded as quickly as he could: his itinerary noting that he came to Caebach and Rhayader on September 29th, before spending the following day with the Jones family, now at Pencerrig. The following month, on October 27th, he was at Pencerrig again and two days later, on the 29th October 1769, he noted: *'To Caebach Meeting House past ten. Found a large congregation gathered and singing in the Meeting House and in the churchyard and strong gales of life… I met many that had been awakened through me in these parts 30 years ago.'*

Howell Harris' personal connection with the Jones family is still strong; a full thirty years after he was rescued by Thomas Jones at the Assizes in 1740, he writes in his diary on Tuesday 17th April 1770: *'At Pencerrig… went with Mr. Jones to Caebach, eight miles from Builth. Discoursed at Caebach…'*

John Thomas repaid Howell Harris for his support by preaching at Trefecca the same month, and again in June. He even stayed there for a fortnight with his wife in November of that year, preaching a sermon there to Harris' followers, every day. For his part, Harris noted that he was again at Caebach on July 3rd of the same year, prior to spending some time at Pencerrig the following day.

By the close of 1771 Harris' health was beginning to fail and his notes show that he proposed a scheme to pay John Thomas for the selling of Welsh devotional books in towns and fairs, John Thomas being a fairly prolific writer of prose, poems and of course, hymns. Again John Thomas is listed as one of the preachers at Trefecca that November.

In 1772, there is another letter from John Thomas, inviting Howell Harris to come again to Caebach – possibly in the face of some opposition: *'One proof that I have that the Lord is still with me, is seeing the devil a-roaring against me in several ways... Sometimes when I open my mouth many of the Carnal people seem to be frightened and run out of the house in great haste...men in general love not plain dealings.'*

However, Harris' health no longer allowed him to travel. He died in 1773, exhausted after a lifetime of travelling and preaching. Four years later, John Thomas left Caebach blaming a *'woman of weak intellect'* in the congregation, who had been consorting with the Baptists; but he continued his ministry in Rhaeadr and Y Garn, **no doubt still supported financially by the Jones family of Pencerrig**. But as the eighteenth century drew to a close, big changes were afoot.

Hannah's husband, Thomas Jones died in 1782. The eldest son John, died in 1787, and as we know, the estate passed into the hands of the next son, Thomas Jones the artist, who by his own admission, had had a rather colourful personal life. He had returned to live at Pencerrig along with his Danish wife Maria, whom he had met whilst in Italy, and their two daughters.

Madam Hannah Jones herself died in Brecon at the home of her younger son Frederick in Brecon, on 19 November 1789. A year earlier, on 10 November 1788, she had endowed her beloved Caebach with the farmhouse and fields surrounding the chapel and an estate of some 37 and a half acres called Carreguan in Llansantffraid in Elfael. According to her request, John Thomas was invited back to Caebach to preach her memorial sermon. His sermon, preached here on 20th of December 1789 was entitled 'Christ the Believer's Life' based on Philippians Chapter 1, verse 21, **'For me to live is Christ, to die is gain'**. The sermon, which became a rather celebrated text, was probably preached in English.

But there was a big problem. Although the sermon was fulsome in its praise for Madam Jones herself, in which he proclaimed that he 'doubted not that our dear sister now deceased', was now 'a member of the glorious society above', in his usual rather tactless fashion, with scant regard for pastoral sensitivities of the grieving family,

John Thomas took the opportunity to remind the six surviving adult Jones offspring, the five sons (all Justices of the Peace) of, to his mind, the consequences of not sharing the same fervent religious beliefs of their parents. That's a diplomatic way of putting it; they didn't see it quite like that. To them, and to one of them, Middleton Jones in particular, it appeared that he had launched a full-scale public censure on them and on their way of life. He was incensed.

If you can imagine this chapel packed to the rafters with family and friends, members, people from the local community, sitting where you are now, and they all heard John Thomas launch forth thus:

"But shall I address myself to the offspring of pious parents? They are gone and you are left. They have laboured and you have entered into their labour... they have left a large portion of this world between you. Remember you are but stewards and yet a little while and you must give account of your stewardship when you are no more stewards.

But O shall we have room to hope that some of you at least will enter into their labours in a far better and higher sense by reaping their examples, prayers and admonitions; in having Christ to be the life of your souls and tread in their steps as far as they followed Christ."

Typical of Methodist preaching he ramps it up and continues:

"You who have not Christ your life, death will be your loss. Death unto you will be a king of terror indeed and will make an end of all your comforts and good things; it will be an open door unto you into endless misery and torments. How will your souls tremble in parting out of the body when you will open your eyes in another world and see your eternal home among devils and the damned in hell? Now you will be stripped of all your former pleasures and all the mercies you enjoyed."

And it didn't stop there. Just in case anyone forgot about it, John Thomas had the sermon in memory of Madam Jones printed at the Trefecca printing press: it came out in 1791, accompanied by a Welsh language version, translated most probably by John Thomas himself. There it was, to be spread abroad in both languages. It is worth noting that during the same year that the sermon was published, Thomas Jones the Artist was appointed High Sheriff of Radnorshire.

The publication understandably angered Middleton Jones even more, and he took action to permanently oust John Thomas from the house provided for him by his mother. Through some legal sleight of hand, he also managed to deprive the chapel of the surrounding farmhouse and fields, an act described by the Revd. Jonathan Williams in his Manuscripts for his History of Radnorshire in 1810 as 'avarice and intolerance' in his treatment of Caebach chapel. John Thomas left the area entirely around 1794 and returned to his native Carmarthenshire and it is unknown what became of him. Some suggest he died in the workhouse at Carmarthen around 1706; other sources suggest he died in Abergwili in 1811, a year after the publication of Rhad Ras. He published and translated a number of Welsh religious works and wrote long elegies to Howell Harris and his wife and Peter Williams, among others. His volume Rhad Ras stands as the first and one of the most powerful first-hand accounts of the Methodist Revival in Wales.

I think it's important to point out that all of the Jones children really did quite well for themselves: David became the vicar of Gladestry near Knighton; Michael went to train to be a surgeon; Frederick developed a successful career with the East India Company; Middleton became a lawyer; and Thomas of course became an artist. But to the mind of John Thomas, they were all eternally lost. Interestingly, there is an entry early the following year in the notebook of Thomas Jones the artist dated 12 March 1792, where he records that he *'Gave his brother Rhys toward the new house at Caebach £9 and 9 shillings.'* Unfortunately, it does not specify whether this refers to a new minister's house for the chapel, or is a reference towards the rebuilding of the chapel which took place in 1804. There is a suggestion that it refers to a new farmhouse and that the material from the original farmhouse was used in the subsequent rebuilding of the chapel.

In fairness to Middleton Jones, he did not deprive the chapel of the Carreguon endowment; in the Powys Archives there is a document dated 19th February 1816 whereby Middleton Jones transfers the Trusteeship on other family members, all to make certain that the Carreguan endowment continues to benefit the chapel.

With the death of Hannah, the family connection and the Methodist connection at Caebach came to an end; but many of their sixteen children are buried in the family vault here, including Thomas Jones the artist.

Who would have thought that this quiet congregational chapel was actually during the eighteenth century a veritable hotbed of Methodist activity and visited over many years by Howell Harris himself.

'God rest the souls of these brave men who faced persecution, ridicule and even penury for their fervent beliefs in bring the message of God's saving grace to a largely disinclined community.

'It is good that we are still remembering them today. As John Thomas himself wrote in one of his most famous and oft sung Welsh hymns:

> *'Am fod fy Iesu'n fyw − byw hefyd fydd ei saint.*
> *Er gorfod dioddef poen a briw, mawr yw eu braint.*
>
> *Because Jesus is alive his saints will also live*
> *even though they had to suffer pain and hurt,*
> *now they have the greatest privilege.'*

I think we need some of this courage to stand up and be counted nowadays. There are so many wonderful people praying for Revival but of course it is all in the Lord's timing. There have been many prophecies that it will start in Wales.

Hannah Jones was the niece of Jones Hope of Llandrindod Wells, 1st cousin of
Anne Jones of Cribarth, who was the 2nd wife of Evan Thomas of Llwyn Madoc 1702-1780

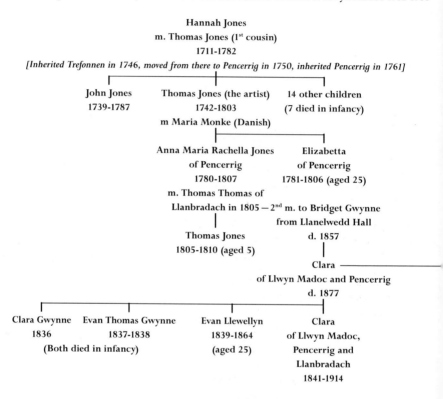

Hannah Jones
m. Thomas Jones (1ˢᵗ cousin)
1711-1782
[Inherited Trefonnen in 1746, moved from there to Pencerrig in 1750, inherited Pencerrig in 1761]

John Jones
1739-1787

Thomas Jones (the artist)
1742-1803
m Maria Monke (Danish)

14 other children
(7 died in infancy)

Anna Maria Rachella Jones
of Pencerrig
1780-1807
m. Thomas Thomas of
Llanbradach in 1805 —

Elizabetta
of Pencerrig
1781-1806 (aged 25)
2ⁿᵈ m. to Bridget Gwynne
from Llanelwedd Hall

Thomas Jones
1805-1810 (aged 5)

d. 1857

Clara
of Llwyn Madoc and Pencerrig
d. 1877

Clara Gwynne
1836

Evan Thomas Gwynne
1837-1838
(Both died in infancy)

Evan Llewellyn
1839-1864
(aged 25)

Clara
of Llwyn Madoc,
Pencerrig and
Llanbradach
1841-1914

THE LLWYN MADOC FAMILY

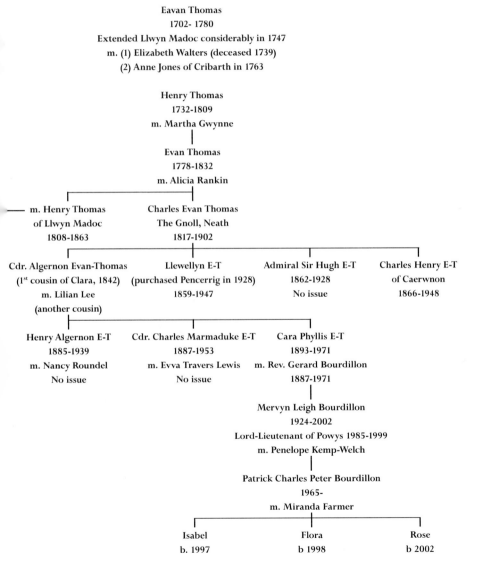

Eavan Thomas
1702- 1780
Extended Llwyn Madoc considerably in 1747
m. (1) Elizabeth Walters (deceased 1739)
(2) Anne Jones of Cribarth in 1763

Henry Thomas
1732-1809
m. Martha Gwynne

Evan Thomas
1778-1832
m. Alicia Rankin

m. Henry Thomas   Charles Evan Thomas
of Llwyn Madoc   The Gnoll, Neath
1808-1863   1817-1902

Cdr. Algernon Evan-Thomas   Llewellyn E-T   Admiral Sir Hugh E-T   Charles Henry E-T
(1st cousin of Clara, 1842)   (purchased Pencerrig in 1928)   1862-1928   of Caerwnon
m. Lilian Lee   1859-1947   No issue   1866-1948
(another cousin)

Henry Algernon E-T   Cdr. Charles Marmaduke E-T   Cara Phyllis E-T
1885-1939   1887-1953   1893-1971
m. Nancy Roundel   m. Evva Travers Lewis   m. Rev. Gerard Bourdillon
No issue   No issue   1887-1971

Mervyn Leigh Bourdillon
1924-2002
Lord-Lieutenant of Powys 1985-1999
m. Penelope Kemp-Welch

Patrick Charles Peter Bourdillon
1965-
m. Miranda Farmer

Isabel   Flora   Rose
b. 1997   b 1998   b 2002